SOUTHEND'S PALACES

of the

SILVER SCREEN

*A History of the Southend Area Cinemas
from Shoeburyness to Canvey Island*

Best wishes

Roy Dilley

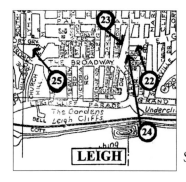

CINEMA
LOCATIONS
(Southend, Westcliff, Leigh, Southchurch and Shoeburyness)

1. Criterion, Palace of Varieties.
2. Rivoli.
3. Kursaal.
4. Princes Picturedome.
5. Civic News Theatre.
6. Gaumont.
7. Theatre De Luxe.
8. Strand.
9. Gem.
10. Garons.
11. Pier Hill Cinema.
12. Regal.
13. Odeon.
14. Ritz.
15. Plaza.
16. Star.
17. Cliffs Pavilion.
18. Kings.
19. Palace Theatre.
20. Mascot.
21. Metropole.
22. Corona.
23. Empire Palace.
24. Henry's Hall.
25. Coliseum.
26. Palace.

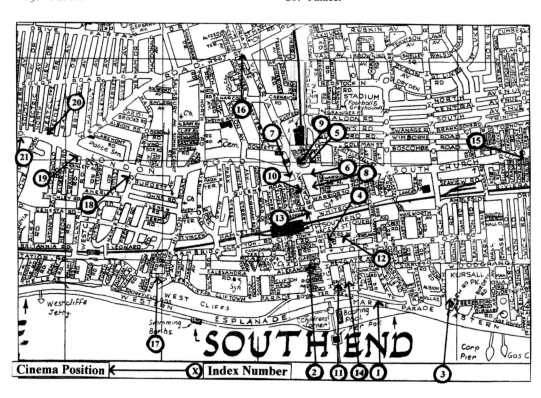

SOUTHEND'S PALACES
of the
SILVER SCREEN

A History of the Southend Area Cinemas
from Shoeburyness to Canvey Island

ROY DILLEY

PHILLIMORE

2011
Published by
PHILLIMORE & CO. LTD
Andover, Hampshire, England
www.phillimore.co.uk

© Roy Dilley, 2011

ISBN 978-1-86077-680-9

Printed and bound in Great Britain
Manufactured by Jellyfish Print Solutions Ltd

This book
is dedicated
to Trish –
my inspiration!

CONTENTS

LIST OF ILLUSTRATIONS

Frontispiece – Maps of Cinema Locations.

Front cover image: Odeon, Southend, 1964.

ILLUSTRATION ACKNOWLEDGEMENTS

My sincere thanks to the following people and organisations for consenting to the use of their photographs.

Glen Chapman, 44; Michael Dedman, 78-80; Roy Dilley, 5, 12, 18, 22, 29, 45-7, 52-3, 57, 66-7, 70, 77, 81, 84, 86-7; Essex Record Office (Chelmsford), 9, 10, 14 (D/BC 1/4/10/9/52), 50 (D/BC 1/4/10/23/84), 58 (D/BC 1/4/10/26/57); M. Hansford, 13; Ernie Johnston, 85; David Keddie, 27-8; Lawrence May, 51; Picture Show, 1-2; Sheila Pitt-Stanley, 76; Rank Leisure Services, front cover, 36, 42-3; Andre Nikola-Smith, 33-5; *Southend Pictorial*, 32; *Southend Standard*, 15-16, 19, 23, 26, 37, 39-41, 49, 59, 61-2; *Southend Times*, 3, 11, 17, 25, 30-1, 55, 68-9; *Southend & Westcliff Graphic*, 6-8, 20-1, 24, 48, 54, 56, 71-5; Ron Stewart, 82-3; Kevin Wheelan, 4, 38, 60, 63-5.

I would like to thank Newsquest Essex for allowing me to reproduce photographs from the *Southend Standard* and *Southend Pictorial* newspapers.

ACKNOWLEDGEMENTS

I would like to give sincere thanks to the following people and organisations for their help in the preparation of this book:

Mrs J. Bousfield
Miss F. Bridge
Glen Chapman
Mike Davies
Michael Dedman
Essex Record Office (Chelmsford)
Mr A.L. Foreman
Bob Grimwood
M. Hansford
Ashley Hitchcock
Mr B. Hodgkinson
Ernie Johnston
David Keddie
Roger Marlow
Lawrence May
Andre Nikola-Smith
Newsquest Essex
Picture Show

Sheila Pitt-Stanley
Mr J.H. Radford
Rank Leisure Services
Mrs E. Raven
Rayleigh Library
Southend Library (& Staff of the Local Studies Dept)
Southend Pictorial
Southend Standard
Southend Times
Southend & Westcliff Graphic
Mr A.P. Steed
Ron Stewart
Rosalind Stratton
Chris Taylor
Kevin Wheelan
Arthur Woodward

Without your kind help with information, or consent to the reproduction of photographs this book could not have been written – thank you all!

INTRODUCTION

I was nearly 14 years old when in 1957 my parents suddenly decided to move to Eastwood from North London. I felt very sad at the thought of leaving my friends behind and probably not seeing them again in the future. Also I would not see our local cinemas again, where I had spent so many hours of my childhood.

Right from the first time my mother had taken me to the Gaumont, at North Finchley, to see *Bambi*, I was hooked, completely lost in a magic world, and this enthusiasm for the cinema has never faded, although a visit to today's multiplex picture houses is a very different experience from cinema-going 50 years ago.

Even at a young age, a visit to the cinema did not only consist of seeing the films; in the intermissions I liked to gaze around the auditoriums, amazed at the architecture which had been so lovingly put into these palaces of entertainment. The beautiful sweeping curves of the art deco Odeon at North Finchley, the sheer luxurious beauty of the Ritz at Muswell Hill, and my lovely Gaumont, at North Finchley, where I had spent all my Saturday mornings watching those thrilling serials! How could I leave all this behind and move to Eastwood?

When we did arrive here and I realised there were so many cinemas around the Southend area, things didn't seem such a catastrophe after all. My first local cinema excursion was to the Southend Essoldo, to see Jayne Mansfield in the rock 'n' roll film *The Girl Can't Help It*. My father was far from keen to see this film, but he didn't say much when we came out of the cinema. I knew he had not liked the music, but I got the impression he hadn't minded Jayne Mansfield too much!

I spent many happy hours in the Essoldo and it became my favourite local cinema. I loved the very big Cinemascope screen and the impressive stereophonic sound the cinema had been fitted with. I recall being there one afternoon watching the film *The Killer Shrews*, when an elderly couple making their way down the aisle managed to fall over the house cat. Luckily, neither of the people nor the cat was hurt in the incident, but it did not help the dramatic atmosphere of the film.

Many of my cinema visits in those days were in the afternoons as Wednesdays were half days where I worked. One such afternoon I had gone to the Ritz to see the film *Ten Seconds From Hell*, starring Jack Palance and Jeff Chandler. While waiting for the film to start an elderly man came and sat in the end seat in the row in front. After a few minutes the lights dimmed and the show commenced. After a while a couple of other people came into the same row where this man was sitting, then a little later the usherette was with this man and shining her torch under and between the rows of seats. I could hear disgruntled murmurings as she said to the man 'Why don't you be more careful', and he replied 'Well it's not my fault'. On the way out I asked the usherette what had happened with this man, she said, 'Well, after the film had been on a while, he had decided to make himself more comfortable, so he removed his teeth and put them in his lap. Some time later a couple of people had come into the row and he had stood up to let them pass, in doing so his teeth had fallen on the floor and they had kicked them along the row'.

My first visit to the dear old Mascot cinema at Westcliff was for an afternoon showing of Donald Wolfit in *Blood of the Vampire*, and Brigitte Bardot in *Love Is My Profession*. This screening was witnessed by myself and just a couple of other people. At the end of the performance, a little elderly lady, sitting in front, turned to me and said quite sternly, 'I think they should be banned'! I was not sure whether she was referring to the two films, or Miss Bardot's main assets, which had been somewhat on display during the afternoon.

While researching this book I have been very aware of two things. Firstly, the real importance these cinema buildings had originally, not only to the lives of people in the days before television, when cinema was the main entertainment, but also the importance to the social structure of the town. Secondly, and very sadly, I was shocked by the almost indecent haste there has been in recent times to demolish these fine buildings.

Developers are only interested in making money, and have no interest in the history or importance of buildings they destroy in the process. Also I feel successive local councils have had little interest in saving the town's history. The Ritz was a magnificent building which would have made a lovely theatre and should never had been demolished. Garons should have had a protection order placed on it; the building had all the original plasterwork from 1911, and would have made an ideal museum. Even though the interior of the Corona at Leigh has been altered, it still retains much of its original plasterwork, dedicated to the Leigh fishing industry. This is another building which ought to be protected.

Each of us has memories of these wonderful buildings, which have provided us all with so many fantastic years of being entertained by the stars of the silver screen. Great days they were indeed. We truly had iconic film stars, starring in well-made films, which the big studios took a pride in making, and we could enjoy all this in the comfort of these beautiful palaces of dreams.

I would like to thank all the various people who have contributed to this book with their recollections and memories. I feel these are an interesting, important and often amusing part of our cinema history, and I was pleased to include them. I would also like to thank all the people and organisations that very kindly consented to allow me to reproduce their photographic material.

Twenty-six years ago I wrote my first book on local cinema history – *The Dream Palaces of Southend*. Over the years I have had many requests to produce another book and, having collected a lot more history on our picture houses, I felt now would be a good time to do this. I hope you enjoy this book and it brings back many happy memories of visits to these wonderful palaces of entertainment.

Of the 31 buildings of film entertainment this book covers, the area now only has two multiplex picture houses, the Odeon at Southend, and the Movie Starr on Canvey Island.

THE BIOSCOPE IS BORN

Our Lives are Changed Forever

Most of the earliest Bioscope shows took place not in permanent buildings erected or converted for the purpose, but in fairgrounds and sideshows which travelled from town to town. The wonder of moving pictures, however primitive, was exhibited to an astonished yet eager audience. It would be half a century before their craving for motion picture entertainment began to subside. During that time films would evolve from visits to those fairground Bioscopes, to the provincial 'penny gaffs' and local kinemas, and finally those super cinemas of the 'thirties'.

The majority of towns of substantial size had witnessed early demonstrations of moving picture presentation. Audiences had gazed in wonderment at the flickering images on the screen. Pictures of Queen Victoria riding in a carriage in Hyde Park, or just nondescript subjects, with the films barely a minute long.

Southend's motion picture history started in just such a small but sensational way, when during 1898 moving pictures of the Boer War were projected at the Criterion Palace of Varieties. This building was situated on the seafront, at 16 Marine Parade. Today it is the *Papillon* public house, although much altered from its appearance a century ago.

Soon after those presentations at the Criterion, Southend, like other towns the length and breadth of the country, witnessed the amazing rise of the Bioscope. Incredible as it may now seem, Southend and the surrounding districts have at one time or another seen the opening of no fewer than 31 buildings of cinema entertainment. These buildings can be divided into three main categories:

1. Halls and other buildings converted specifically for film presentation.
2. Theatres converted to picture houses.
3. Purpose-built cinemas.

This book of the Southend area cinema history deals with all the above types of buildings. It does not include assembly halls and other public meeting venues, which presented films (mostly in the early days), as part and parcel of many other uses. This would include the following venues:

The **Pier Pavilion**, Southend, had plans passed for a projection box in 1910, and films were presented for a few years on an intermittent basis. The hall had a seating capacity of 1,200 and was also used for shows, concerts, dancing, skating and many other entertainments.

The **Victoria Hall**, at 48-52 Alexandra Street, Southend, was built in 1879. It had a bioscope box added and showed films in 1909. The hall seated 500, and was also used for plays, social functions, boxing exhibitions, whist drives, concerts and Dances.

The **Public Hall** was built on the London Road at Hadleigh in 1912. It was erected as a general social meeting place. It was used later for film shows and also as a skating rink. The film shows were not held on a regular basis, and an old gas engine at the rear of the building provided power for the projector and lights. Later the hall was used for billiards and darts.

The **Benfleet Kinema** was an all-purpose public hall, situated on the corner of Brook Road and High Road, Benfleet. It presented film shows in the early '20s and later became the Barn Club, with part of the hall being used for billiards.

The **Bohemia Hall** was erected near Small Gains Corner, on Canvey Island, in 1902. It was built as a community hall and later used by Mr Henry Pettitt to show films of Charlie Chaplin, Mary Pickford and Tom Mix. (Mr Pettitt was a former travelling cinema proprietor.)

The **Paddocks**, at Long Road, Canvey Island, is a council owned, all-purpose public hall, which presented films between 11 March 1982 and May 1983. The hall had a seating capacity of 400, on a flat floor. Ross projectors had been installed, together with a 25-foot screen. Unfortunately the venture did not receive enough support to make it a viable enterprise and films were discontinued.

THE CINEMAS SOUTHEND NEARLY HAD

Plans for a proposed **Cinematograph Hall**, at 35 Queens Road, Southend, were submitted to the Council planning office, by J. Kelf & Co., in July 1913. The plans called for the conversion of a building which fronted on to Queens Road, and was situated midway between Elmer Avenue and Napier Avenue. The rear of the building had access to both these roads by passageways.

The architect was Norman Evans of County Chambers, Weston Road, Southend. The plans for the Cinematograph Hall made provision for seating on two levels, the ground-floor seats being mounted on a flat floor. The seats in a small gallery would have been on a sloping floor, with the operating box alongside them. The cinema would have only been able to use non-inflammable films.

The plans were disapproved by the Council planning department, on 1 September 1913, because the walls of the building were of insufficient thickness for the purposes of a public building. The Cinematograph Hall was never constructed.

In November 1910, plans were drawn up for the **Premier Electric Theatre**, which was to be built in Southend's Broadway (now High Street), on the corner of Warrior Square. The building was to be owned by the Premier Electric Company, and had been designed by Mr W.A. Lewis, of Finsbury Square, London.

The ground floor of the building would have covered an area of 150 feet, and shops were to have been erected on either side of the entrance. The plans also provided for a balcony, lounge and restaurant. Although the plans were approved on 19 December 1910, the cinema was never built, Boot's chemist shop later occupied the site, which more recently has been Principles shop. A century after being built the exterior has altered little, and if you look at the top of the building's frontage you can still see the dome and central rising façade, which were part of the original cinema plans.

On 17 May 1913, plans were submitted to the building inspector's office for the erection of an **Electric Theatre**, in Southchurch Road. This was to be situated on the north side of the road, near the junction with Ilfracombe Road. The owner would be Mr R.N. Nerney, of Boston Avenue, Southend (Mr Nerney was also managing director of the Southend-on-Sea Theatre Co. Ltd, who owned the Empire theatre, Southend).

The architect of the Electric Theatre was Laurence T. Weaser, and the picture house would have a seating capacity of 814. After agreement to certain amendments the plans were approved on 20 May 1913, but the cinema was never built.

In March 1913, plans were drawn up for the conversion of three houses to form part of a **Cinema Hall**, at 45-49 Leigh Road East (now the London Road). The site of the proposed cinema was on the north side of Leigh Road East, at Westcliff, near the junction with Balmoral Road. The owner was Mr George Lindsay and the architect Mr James Thompson. A committee from the building inspector's office visited the site on 17 March 1913, and the plans were disapproved on 14 April 1913.

On 17 September 1936, it was announced that a super cinema with a seating capacity of 1,900 would be built at Leigh, on a site at the corner of the London Road and Blenheim Crescent. The building would occupy land formerly used as a wood yard and also the site of two houses. An earlier cinema venture had been intended for this site some years previously.

The plans drawn up provided for a fully equipped stage to facilitate variety performances as well as cinema presentations. The picture house would have had every comfort, including cloak rooms and an ample car park; also, shops would have been included in the design of the cinema frontage. There was provision for an organ with a decorative console to be installed in front of the stage, together with space to accommodate an orchestra. A café-ballroom with a sprung dance floor was also included in the plans.

The new house was to be called the **Blenheim Cinema**, and was being designed by Mr F.L. Buckley, of Dale Road, Leigh. The owners were to be the Blenheim Super Cinema Company, whose managing director was Mr J.P. Lewis. It was hoped that building work would commence in December 1936, and the cinema be open by July 1937. Once again the cinema was never built. A block of flats was later erected on the site.

On 16 January 1911, plans were submitted to the building inspector's office for a **Picture Hall** at the rear of 2-3 Marine Parade, at the bottom of Pier Hill, on Southend's seafront. Entrance to the hall would be via a passageway between the two shops. The owner of the proposed hall was Mr W.N. Walters, the architect Bertram Parkes, of Weston Road, Southend, and the builders Pollard & Co. Mr Walters gained permission from the St John's Church authorities for a right of way to the private road at the rear of the hall, which connected to Lucy Road. After further structural alterations to the building, the plans were approved on 6 May 1912.

Plans were submitted on 3 March 1911, for the conversion of a house and shop into a cinematograph hall at 143 Victoria Avenue, Prittlewell. The owner was Mr C.R. Brown, and the bioscope would be named the **Prittlewell Electric Theatre**. A lock-up shop would be retained at the front of the building, next to the cinema's entrance vestibule and pay box. The operating box would be at the back of the building, with a rear projection unit being installed. The plans were approved on 3 April 1911.

Here we have a mystery! In over 30 years of researching Southend's cinema history, I have never seen an advertisement, article, or any reference at all, to either of the above two Pictures Halls, so there is no proof that they were ever constructed or opened, even though the plans had been approved by the Council Building Office.

Normally I would conclude they were two more cinematograph buildings which were planned but never built. However, an elderly lady I knew over 30 years ago was certain that there had been Bioscope presentations at these two locations. I can only hope that sometime in the future I may be able to establish positively that this is correct.

RIVOLI

Southend

The Public Hall was built in Alexandra Street in 1872. It was one of the first public buildings to be erected in the town, and owed its origins to the spirit of enterprise for which Alderman Hemmann was well known. He felt the building was a sign of better things for the town, but it had a chequered existence. Its erection and management were entrusted to a public company, which, sorry to say, rarely flourished. In March 1877, early projected screen entertainment took place at the Public Hall, presented by Mr William Catlin. 'Round the World in 90 Minutes' was a presentation of dissolving views, projected onto a screen 20 feet in diameter, by the new oxy-hydrogen lime light. The programme included views of the Rocky Mountains, Salt Lake City and the great fire of Chicago.

By 1886, the name of the building had been changed to the Alexandra Theatre. One of the shows presented in March that year was Millar's Electoscopic Diorama, a two-hour show, with magnificent scenes of the Sudan war and General Gordon at Khartoum, combined with marvellous mechanical effects. Sadly, through the years financial results at the theatre did not improve. After many ups and downs, in 1894 the building was put up to auction, but failed to gain a purchaser, and was afterwards privately sold to Mr William Fred Marlow, who lived at 89 Milton Street, Southend.

Fred Marlow (as he was usually known), was a leading London entrepreneur, actor, theatre manager and builder, who gave his name to Marlow's Palace of Varieties, in Bow. Fred set about converting the bleak Alexandra Theatre into a lavish place of entertainment, renaming it the Empire Theatre. The building needed in the region of £10,000 to be spent on renovation. A gallery was erected, and the auditorium was re-seated and re-fitted. The work had only just finished, when, in the bitterly cold early hours of 6 January 1895, the theatre was completely destroyed by fire, in spite of determined efforts by the Southend Fire Brigade, police and helpers.

The fire had been discovered at 2.10 a.m. by police officers on duty in the area. A smell of smoke in the air was detected and then located to the theatre. These police officers, by means of fire bells, alarmed the Fire Brigade but, in the eight minutes it took the firemen to arrive, flames began to appear through the roof. Within a very short time the flames shot up to immense heights and ran along to the other end of the building. The heat grew so intense that the lead flashing and guttering on the roof melted and ran down the side of the building.

The police, in their few minutes of waiting for the Fire Brigade, aroused William Heffer, who, as caretaker, was sleeping in a room on the ground floor of the theatre. On being awakened, he sat up and rubbing his eyes said, 'Fire, what fire?' The police then conducted him in his nightshirt across the road to the police station opposite, where he dressed. Inhabitants of the buildings both sides of the theatre were made aware of their risk, and some were taken across – all scantily attired – to the police station, while others began to remove their belongings into the street. At 3.30 a.m. the roof of the building fell in, and by then the only remaining portions of the building were the four walls and the main ground-floor entrance. It took some hours to extinguish the blaze completely, and by then all that remained was a roofless ruin. A discarded cigarette was later suspected to be the cause of the fire.

But Fred Marlow was not a man to be beaten by a small thing such as his theatre being totally destroyed. A few days after the fire, the theatre façade collapsed into the street below, while demolition work was in progress. Those in the street had to run for their lives. The man responsible was Fred, who had been helping demolish the building himself, and pushed the façade the wrong way!

Fred rebuilt the theatre, at a cost of £25,000, and the magnificent Empire Theatre rose from the ashes of the former building. At one time it looked as if the building would not be finished for the Whit Bank Holiday, but through the energy of Fred Marlow (he having personally supervised the whole of the work himself), the structure was completed in time. The Empire seated 2,000 people, half of whom could be seated in the gallery. Six private boxes overlooked the stage, and sloping up behind the 150 orchestral stalls were about 500 pit seats, a special floor being set apart for the dress and upper circles which seated 300. The seating was arranged semi-circular and upholstered in plum coloured plush. The ceiling and the tinting of the wall decorations were in light blue, gold and salmon pink relief. The stage was on a scale to accommodate the largest touring companies in the country. The interior was delightful. Mr Marlow had presented his patrons with a theatre to satisfy the needs of Southend for the next quarter of a century.

The new theatre opened on Monday, 25 May 1896. The opening ceremony took place to a well filled theatre. The band, under Mr Harry Read, opened with an overture, after which the Mayor Councillor Prevost congratulated Mr Marlow on building the theatre and hoped it would be full at all future performances. He said that he considered this theatre vied with any London theatre in existence, and added that there need not be any fear from fire, for the justices had been very particular and had looked over the theatre thoroughly. The many exits and fire extinguishing apparatus showed that due regard had been given to the safety of patrons. The Mayor then asked his good friend, Major Rasch, to open the grand and magnificent theatre. Major Rasch also congratulated Mr Marlow on the splendid building, and declared the Empire Theatre open to the public.

1 *The Rivoli pictured in 1923.*

Fred Marlow was already a very popular man in Southend. His appearance on the stage that evening at the opening ceremony was a signal for tremendous cheers. He told the audience: 'I hope all of you will enjoy the performance. As long as I am among you, I hope you will like me. At the laying of the foundation stone I promised that I would build you

2   *Interior of the Rivoli in 1923.*

one of the prettiest theatres in the United Kingdom, and have I not kept my word?' The evening then continued with the performance of 'Maritana', performed by Neilson's Grand English Opera Company.

Fred remained owner of the theatre until 1905, when it became the property of the Southend Theatre Company. Fred Marlow went on to build houses in Southend, as well as running entertainments at the Pier Pavilion and becoming a councillor.

In April, 1909, Adam Seebold took over as managing director of the Empire. After many years of financial problems and various lessees, the Empire Theatre closed on 9 August 1919 and the last production was 'The Luck Of The Navy'. The building was about to be transformed into the palatial Rivoli cinema, owned by the Rivoli Cinema Co. Ltd, of Finsbury Park, London.

There had been no small amount of speculation amongst the groups of people who had watched the transformation of the theatre into the impressive Rivoli cinema, as to whether the scene would be complete for the opening ceremony, advertised for 17 May. Workmen had seemingly swarmed over and under the building for weeks, and there had been night shifts and Sunday labour. Ultimately the contractors won the race against time, and there stood Southend's latest palace of dreams, a credit to the management and no mean acquisition to the town.

The cinema seated 1,500 in comfortable 'tip up'-style seats. There were two balconies, the first consisting of convenient family boxes. Apart from the fact it stood on the same site, the Rivoli had no connection with the old Empire. Inside, it was an impossibility to 'fix' the former building. The painters were most lavish with the gold paint on the proscenium decorations, which were a marvellous piece of handiwork. A two-manual pipe organ, costing £118, had been installed, and the building had a café over the entrance vestibule. To obviate the possibility of interruption through failure of the electric current, a special generating plant had been installed.

The opening ceremony on 17 May 1920 was performed by the Mayor (Ald. F.W. Senier), who was accompanied by the Mayoress. The building was well filled with invited guests. After the Mayoress had received a handsome bouquet and the Mayor a Presentation key, the latter said he congratulated those responsible for the marvellous manner in which they had transformed the building into the spacious and really handsome cinema. In declaring the Rivoli open, he expressed his best wishes for its future success, and introduced resident manager Mr Leonard A. Boulter to the audience. The company then watched the film *A Daughter of Eve*, and tea followed. The Rivoli opened to the public on 31 May, with the films *Flame of Life* and *A Little Child Shall Lead Them*. In 1921, the Rivoli became part of Sidney Bacon's small circuit of cinemas, his monogram in gilt letters were inscribed over the proscenium arch.

On 26 July 1923, the *Southend Standard* reported;

Extra Turn at the Rivoli. Prompt action on the part of the firemen of the Rivoli cinema, subdued an outbreak of fire caused by a fuse, on Saturday at 9.40 p.m. The programme had an hour to run, when one of the red curtains at the side of the proscenium burst into flames. The screen was soon alight and just as soon the cinema firemen were playing on it with a hose. Naturally, some excitement prevailed amongst the packed audience, but any danger of panic was averted by the orchestra. They struck up a lively tune, though water was pouring down upon them at the time. Many members were drenched, the cornet player, thoroughly soaked and slightly scorched, came along with a solo 'I'm Forever Blowing Bubbles', an item which was loudly applauded. The businesslike methods of the fire fighters were also cheered and when the Southend Fire Brigade arrived their services were not required. During operations one of the attendants, Mr J.H. Richardson, of Shaftesbury Avenue, clambered up one of the curtains to deal with a section of the fire. After he had gone about twelve feet up he lost his grip and fell. Taken to Victoria Hospital he was detained with an injury to his back. It was possible for everyone to have left the building through a large number of exits, but few took fright, the majority remaining to see the 'extra turn'. The manager Mr Chamberlain controlled everything well and after an assuring speech from him, the audience left. A new screen was rigged up for the Sunday evening performance.

Amongst the great silent films shown at the Rivoli was Lon Chaney in *The Hunchback Of Notre Dame* and Ramon Navarro in *Ben Hur*. Also many of the Tom Mix and Buck Jones westerns were screened. On occasions, to add to the drama of the film, electrically operated explosions were set off on the side of the stage, to coincide with blowing up a ship or castle, etc.

Mr A.L. Foreman remembers:

For a time, as in many cinemas during a period, stage shows were part and parcel of the entertainment. One of the artists I can recall seeing was Ronald Frankau, of BBC radio fame.

During 1928, the original organ was removed, and replaced with a two manual Christie, which was inaugurated by Wilson Oliphant.

On 30 August 1929, Sidney Bacon announced that shortly sound films would be shown at the Rivoli. The sound equipment had been purchased, and he felt it would be delivered and installed by October. Mr Bacon said he wanted the Rivoli to be the first Southend cinema to put on 'talkies'. He realised that the first cinema in the town to do so would draw immense audiences, although he felt one of the other local cinemas may try to beat his October date.

A Western Electric Sound system was installed, and the Rivoli became the first cinema in Southend to present sound films (beating Garons cinema by seven days), when, on 7 October 1929, *The Broadway Melody*, starring Charles King and Anita Page, was presented and billed as 'The Screen Event of the Year'.

In 1936, the cinema was completely modernised and decorated after becoming part of the Union circuit, re-opening on 28 December, with a seating capacity of 1,369. A three-manual Wurlitzer organ had been installed which was played by Harold Ramsey, and was later also played by Peggy Webber and Neville Meale. This instrument remained in the cinema until 1959. The Rivoli became part of the A.B.C. circuit in 1937, when Union was taken over by Associated British Cinemas. The Rivoli switched their programme change day from Sunday to Thursday on 3 June 1954.

3   *The 'talkie' equipment arrives at the Rivoli.*

4   *After modernisation, the Rivoli in 1936.*

The cinema closed on 4 November 1961 for six-and-a-half months, the picture house being completely modernised and re-decorated at a cost of £90,000. The building now had a completely redesigned front elevation, of golden brown brickwork with mosaic and marble briquette. The new foyer was brilliantly lit, with ultra modern-style pay box and sales kiosk.

On entering the auditorium, it was quickly seen that the emphasis had been put on comfort. The sweeping proscenium opening had been draped in oyster-coloured curtains, set against black and gold wallpaper. The balcony had been extended forward; this major redesign served to affect a more intimate atmosphere. The cinema had been equipped with the very latest seating, providing the highest degree of comfort, with ample knee-room and ease of access. The seating had been reduced to 1,226. Carpet throughout the auditorium was a high quality Wilton, in pleasing and colourful designs, which also blended with the general décor. A new and highly efficient heating and ventilation plant had been installed, which constantly changed the air, thermostatically controlling it at a comfortable temperature. The latest type of projectors had been installed and also the newest type of cinema screen, which ensured that all pictures were projected under perfect conditions.

The luxury cinema reopened on 7 June 1962, being renamed A.B.C. The opening ceremony was conducted by the Mayor, Ald. Osborn A. Moss, before a distinguished

5   *The A.B.C. opening week, 1962.*

audience. Film stars Richard Todd, Sylvia Syms, Ronald Fraser and June Richie appeared on the stage of the cinema for the opening ceremony. The re-opening film was *Escape From Zahrain*, starring Yul Brynner.

The A.B.C. was the first cinema in Britain to open a Theatre Club – the Marine Bar. In 1977, the building was fitted out for 'Sensurround' presentations, the first of which was *Rollercoaster*. Massive speakers were bolted to the floor at the rear of the auditorium. At the appropriate sections of the film (the rollercoaster rides), the soundtrack was fed through special amplifiers, into these speakers, so the floor of the auditorium vibrated, to give the effect of the rollercoaster.

On 1 March 1980 the A.B.C. again closed, this time for conversion to twin auditoriums. These opened on 22 May, with A.B.C.1 seating 680 and A.B.C.2 seating 298. The reopening films were *Life of Brian* and *Mission Galactica*. The cinema became the Cannon on 12 December 1986.

Southend has been very fortunate over the years in some very dedicated cinema staff, including some excellent managers. For many years Mrs Lesley Savill had been assistant manager, then manager, at the Classic (later Cannon), cinema at Westcliff. During 1988, Lesley transferred to the Southend Cannon as manager, and was paramount in the continued success of the cinema at a very difficult time. The M.G.M. group which then controlled Cannon cinemas split their cinemas into grades. In 1993, Lesley won a top award as the best manager in her class, and was presented with a silver model of the famous M.G.M. lion. Once again the cinema reverted to the name A.B.C. on 14 June 1996.

The cinema closed on 22 January 1998. The last films were *Starship Troopers*, in A.B.C.1 and *The Jackal* in A.B.C.2. The building reopened on 10 October 1998, after being converted to the New Empire Theatre. The first show was *Little Shop of Horrors*. The New Empire closed on 7 November 2008. Under the modern foyer of the building are some of the original theatre passageways. The walls retain their original decorations, with the conventional hand signs still pointing the way to the pit and stalls.

A year after closure the building has been emptied of a large amount of its contents, and now stands unused. Could this be the end for another of Southend's historic buildings?

KURSAAL

Southend

The Luna Park and Palace was a magnificent structure of brick and iron, surmounted by an imposing glass dome. Facing the sea, the building was situated in the middle of Marine Parade, and easily reached from the High Street. The Luna Park and Palace was erected in 1902, at a cost of £250,000. 1904 saw the opening of Ruffels Imperial Bioscope, when films were first shown in the ballroom, the entrance price being 1d.

By 1910, the bioscope had gained its own hall and was drawing large audiences. Performances were twice nightly at 7 p.m. and 9 p.m. Seats in the body of the hall were 1d. and 3d. The balcony was free (a charge of 1d., to gain entry to the palace and park, had already been paid). The films were up-to-date, and no expense was spared to obtain the very best possible results.

During 1910, a further sum of £50,000 was spent on additions and improvements to the building. The complex then covered about four acres, comprising a large ballroom, in which 2,000 couples could dance at one time (also used as an all-purpose concert hall). The site also included a crystal skating rink, the bioscope and amusement park.

A new cinema auditorium, with a seating capacity of 646, was built in October 1913, and was named the Kursaal Kinema, as the whole complex had now been renamed the Kursaal. According to a later newspaper report, the films would sometimes jump up and down on the screen, where they had been badly joined. But in contrast to later and more critical audiences no one uttered so much as a murmur.

On 14 April 1914 plans were submitted to the building inspector's office for the erection of a Daylight Cinema in the Kursaal grounds, adjoining the rollercoaster. The temporary structure would be 150 feet long, by 40 feet wide and 20 feet high at the front. It would be an open-air cinema, with a 16-foot high screen and a canvas roof. The projection box would be lined with sheet iron. The plans were submitted by the Sunlight Screen Company Ltd, of Piccadilly Circus, London, but were disapproved by the planning office.

The Kinema closed for the First World War, while the Kursaal was used by troops. The auditorium was later redecorated and the Kinema reopened on 26 January 1920 with the film *In Friendship's Name* starring Ruth Clifford. There was a full orchestra, and programmes ran continuously from 6.30 p.m. to 10.30 p.m. The auditorium now had a seating capacity of 1,000.

During 1928, Mr Kinder filmed various events around the town for 'The Kursaal Scrapbook', a local newsreel, which was one of the items presented on the screen. The Kursaal was one of the last cinemas in the borough to install 'talkie' apparatus, but on 10 October 1930 the Kinema announced that they 'Could stay silent no longer'. A Western Electric Sound system had been installed. The loudspeaker from this system was said to be the largest in Southend. The first sound film presented was *Sunny Side Up*, starring Janet Gaynor and Charles Farrell, shown on 13 October. The advertisements

6   *Entrance of the Kursaal.*

proudly stated that there was no increase in admission charges. The Kursaal was the first local cinema to show 'British Movietone News'. The Kinema had Simplex projectors. The

7   *The new Kinema auditorium under construction in 1913.*

8   *Full house at the Kursaal Kinema, 1913.*

automatic shutter control, which enabled an instantaneous changeover between the two projectors, was achieved by a foot switch, the only system of its kind in the borough.

In July 1940, the following notice appeared in the *Southend Times* newspaper: 'In thanking our patrons for their past support, we regret to announce that, owing to the prevailing circumstances, this cinema will be closed as from Saturday next, 20th July'. The last film shown at the Kursaal Kinema was Ginger Rogers and David Niven in *Bachelor Mother*, supported by *The Spellbinder* starring Lee Tracy and Barbara Read. The former cinema became the Estuary Room, a banqueting suite.

Much of the Kursaal declined through the years and became disused. Most of the complex was demolished in 1987, and houses were erected on the site of the amusement park. The front part of the Kursaal building remains, accommodating a casino, bowling alley and café.

PRINCES PICTUREDOME

Southend

The Princes Hall was built in 1896, at the rear of the *London Public House*, in Tylers Avenue. The hall cost £1,200 to construct and seated 400. In 1906 the owner was Arthur Schrynemaker.

Originally the hall presented variety, but by 1908 this had altered to a mixture of variety and bioscope shows, twice nightly at 6.50 p.m. and 8.50 p.m., matinées Wednesdays and Saturdays at 2.30 p.m. Popular prices were Gallery 2d. – Early Door 3d., Pit 4d. – Early Door 6d., Pit Stalls 6d. – Early Door 9d., Stalls 9d. – Early Door or booked 1/-. Early doors opened at 6.15 p.m. and 8.30 p.m.

After a short closure, the building reopened on 16 September 1910 as a cinema, being renamed the Princes Picturedrome. The adverts proclaimed: 'This select and up-to-date Picturedrome is now open daily 2.30 p.m. to 10.45 p.m., Sundays 5 p.m. to 9.45 p.m. Admission prices are 2d., 4d., and 6d. We are the only picture entertainers placing a complete change of programme every day before the public'. The hall had been entirely re-seated and re-decorated.

The *Southend Graphic* newspaper stated:

The Bioscope entertainment is the best of its kind. The films are not only new, but entirely free from flickering. The programmes are excellently balanced, and

9   *The Princes Picturedrome, 1914.*

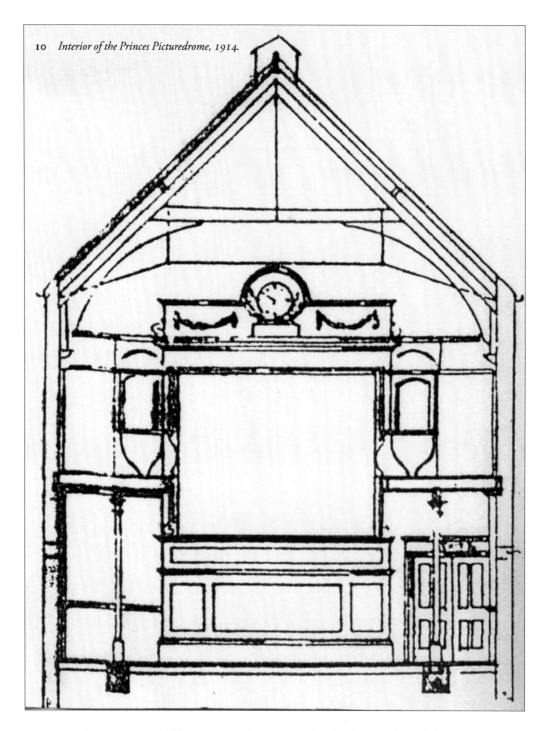

10 *Interior of the Princes Picturedrome, 1914.*

the introduction of topical films is eminently praiseworthy, also the inclusion of Pathe's animated 'Gazette'. The performances are continuous, and there is no waiting. The transformed hall is now one of the most comfortable in the borough, and has the reputation of producing the clearest and steadiest pictures ever thrown on to a sheet.

In 1912, the cinema closed again, and was partly reconstructed and artistically decorated, reopening on 10 May. The special attraction that week was a fine film of the Titanic disaster. The Picturedrome now possessed a spacious balcony, increasing the seating capacity to five hundred. The programme was changed four times weekly. Music was supplied by an orchestra after 6 p.m. In 1914 the advertisements stated: 'Free tea from 3 p.m. daily and at night cups of French coffee are given to visitors'.

In 1920, the name of the cinema changed to the Avenue when it came under the control of Avenue Electric Theatres Ltd., and later Meldrum and Searchfield. The advertisements for 2 February, 1922, announced: 'Now showing to packed houses! Do not miss to-night, the first episode of *Hidden Dangers*, featuring Joe Ryan and Jean Paige'.

The cinema name changed again in 1925 to the Lyric; the lessee was Mr H. Gilder.

When the Mayor's Unemployment Committee met, in the Council Chamber, at Southend, on 6 January 1926 they had received a letter from Mr Gilder, stating that, owing to the abuse offered to his female staff, he could allow no more free tickets to the cinema for the unemployed. The clerk, Mr A. Hutchings, reported he had written to Mr Gilder, expressing his regret. The Chairman, Mr E. Cecil Jones, said he had visited the cinema with the Clerk, because he regarded it as very upsetting that there had been any need for such a letter to be written. Enquiries showed that in a few cases some of the unemployed and

11   *Entrance of the Avenue cinema, 1923.*

their wives had made a little trouble because of the position in which they were asked to sit. It seemed that at the Lyric the two front rows were reserved for the unemployed and their children, and there had been an objection to the seats, because they thought they should sit a little further back, and derogatory remarks had been made to the staff about the cinema.

The picture house finally closed on 23 January 1929. The last films were *A Going Concern*, Albertini in *Thou Shalt Not*, and also a *Bindle Millionaire Comedy*. For many years the site was a car park for the *London Public House*, later *The Tavern in the Town*. More recently Churchill's wine bar has occupied the site.

PIER HILL CINEMA

Southend

Built next to the *Grand Pier Hotel* in Grove Terrace, at the top of Pier Hill, the Southend Picture Palace was opened in June 1909. The owner was Mr R. Arnold. Advertisements in the local press proclaimed: 'Grand Pictorial Concert. Every Seat Upholstered'. On 23 February 1912 the cinema announced, 'The Court Intrigue of Henry VIII, in colour – 3010 feet, plus a naval picture, don't miss the shot through the torpedo tube'.

The name of the building was changed to The Grove Picture Theatre by 1913. The owner was Mr F.F. Ramuz, who also owned the Gem Electric Theatre, at Victoria Circus.

In 1914, the name of the picture house changed again to the Pier Hill Cinema. The owner was now Mr Burgh, who had recently purchased the cinema from Mr Goldberg, and the new lessee was Mr Emmanuel Levy.

On 13 January 1913 Mr Levy appeared at Southend Police Court, before the Mayor, Joseph Francis Esq, who stated that Mr Levy had failed to obtain a music licence for the picture house. Mr Levy replied that he was not aware he needed a music licence. In London, where he had come from, if you only had a piano in the cinema, such a licence was not needed. The Mayor retorted that Mr Levy wasn't in London now and it was his responsibility to find out what licences were necessary. Mr Francis Fisher, appearing for Mr Levy, said that when Mr Burgh purchased the cinema from Mr Goldberg he had made sure the Cinematograph licence was transferred, but had taken no action over the music licence; therefore it was Mr Burgh's fault and not his client's. Police Superintendent Jones stated he had already told Mr Levy and the other parties that the licence needed to be transferred, but no further action had taken place. He added that these people were in and out of these places without giving any notice, and it was often some time before they knew of the change. The Mayor said he was aware the Cinematograph licence had been correctly transferred. Superintendent Jones agreed that had been achieved satisfactorily; personally his only complaint was these people coming in and going out without notice. The Mayor said all he was trying to find out, if he could, who was at fault.

12   *The Grove Picture Theatre in 1914.*

Mr A.P. Steed recalls:

The cinema was very crude and antiquated even in 1916. We used to go to the kids shows on Saturday afternoons. Admission was 1d., and you got an orange or bag of sweets if you behaved yourself, if you didn't you were chucked out.

The building enjoyed a fairly short life as a bioscope, closing in 1919. For a time it was used as a billiard saloon. The site was later developed into part of a coach station (the building next door being the other part), and used by Westcliff Motor Services. In 1981, the site of the former cinema and the surrounding buildings were gradually cleared to make way for the Royals shopping complex.

13   *The Pier Hill Cinema, 1916.*

THEATRE DE LUXE

Southend

Situated in the London Road, near Victoria Circus, the Theatre De Luxe opened during the third week of October 1909. It was owned by Electric Theatres (1908), Ltd, who owned other cinemas in London and the provinces. The directors of this company stated in the opening adverts: 'We beg to announce that we have opened one of our well-known theatres in Southend. The theatre is tastefully decorated, comfortably seated and furnished, and makes a charming rendezvous for the residents of the district. The entertainment is of the same interesting and up-to-date character so favourably known at the company's other theatres, in and around London and the provinces. It consists of the choice selection of animated pictures, dramatic, comic, and travel subjects, also topical events are a special feature.'

Programmes changed every Monday and Thursday, and were continuous from 2 p.m. to 10.30 p.m. The price of admission was adults 3d., and children 2d., and patrons were promised a full hour's entertainment at any time.

The *Southend Graphic* reported;

The Bioscope pictures at the Theatre De Luxe are excellent, and cover a wide field. They range from grave to gay, from lively to serious. Some of the films are highly dramatic. The entertainment is running all the time, and there is no waiting. There is music, and the hall is well heated and comfortable.

In January 1910 the directors of the Theatre De Luxe, through their manager, Mr J.W. Hemming, invited a number of children from the Cripples' Home at Southchurch Beach, and 50 orphans from the Convent Home to witness a bioscope performance. Each child received a bag of sweets, an orange and a mince pie. By February 1910 no fewer than 70,000 people had visited this popular house. The cinema stated in their adverts that they presented the finest cinematograph entertainment in Southend.

14   *The Theatre De Luxe in 1910.*

Mr A.P. Steed recalls:

The Theatre De Luxe was quite narrow and the audience well behaved. My first recollections are the number of times the film broke or caught fire. I spent many happy hours watching Pearl White serials, Ruth Roland and W.S. Hart, around 1915-16. The film was hand cranked and used to go through a hole in the floor to the rewind bay, in a little room below. They showed a lot of British films, made by small companies on a shoe string. Also shown were the bigger Stoll films, and very good they were too – much better than Hollywood.

In 1918, to promote a forthcoming Pearl White serial, the cinema issued a postcard to its patrons. On one side was a picture of Pearl White, on the other side it read: 'Just a line to let you know I am returning to the Theatre De Luxe, Southend, in my latest serial film entitled *the Fatal Ring*. The first episode will be shown on Thursday, 30 May. Serially Yours, Pearl White.'

In 1919, plans were approved for alterations to the auditorium, the left-hand wall would be straightened, and with the addition of a balcony would increase the seating to 820 in the stalls and add a further 210 with the balcony.

On 7 August 1923 the Theatre De Luxe was badly damaged by a fire in the roof.

The *Southend Standard* newspaper reported:

Late on Tuesday night the Theatre De Luxe was partially destroyed by fire, which several hundreds of people, attired in various stages of dress and undress, witnessed. The outbreak was first noted by Police Constable Tomkins, who saw smoke coming from the centre of the roof, as he walked up Queens Road at 10.40 p.m., some fifteen minutes after the conclusion of the performance, and the staff had departed. He ran to Cobweb Corner[1] and broke the glass at the alarm post. Within three minutes the Southend Fire Brigade had arrived with two engines, meanwhile the crowd had collected. Many risked missing the last tram, when it was seen there was a chance of excitement. Hoses lay at every conceivable angle, and small boys enjoyed the fountains which played from the many punctures therein, as much as the fire. Tongues of flame shooting from the cinema's roof lit up the neighbourhood and volumes of smoke rolled away on a slight breeze. There were firemen on the roof of Mr J.F. Dixon's draper's shop next door. In Queens Road the exit doors of the cinema were forced and several hoses were trained upwards to the roof inside. There was great speculation as to whether one of the brigade perched on top of an escape ladder, and working away diligently, was dressed in pyjamas. He was not. It was Ted Johnson, who had just come in from tennis when the alarm was received at Leigh. He was working in flannel trousers with fireman's tunic and helmet. The crowd had grown to thousands now, along with a stream of stopped vehicles in the London Road, as traffic was suspended for an hour. The flames were confined to the roof, and despite the alarming reports of a 'gutted cinema', which appeared the next morning in the London contemporaries, the fire never came below the ceiling, apart from the falling rafters, and these were promptly dealt with. It was the water – forced on the flames at a rate of 1,500 gallons per minute – together with smouldering wood, that rendered most of the seating accommodation impossible for future use. Next morning this usually cosy cinema presented a forlorn appearance, and the downcast faces of the employees as they wandered about the soaked gangways added yet another dismal touch. The sunshine streamed through the charred rafters and, as they dried in the heat, steam rose from the seats. There had been nearly a foot of water all over the floor of the building when

15   *The Theatre De Luxe, 1923, the day after the fire.*

1   Victoria Circus was affectionately known as Cobweb Corner because of the numerous overhead electric tram wires.

the fire was at its height, but this had all subsided. No damage had been done to the screen or to the piano and harmonium just below it. A large placard in front of the pay-box struck an ironical note. It gave the average temperature of the theatre and stated, 'It is 20% cooler inside'. The Fire Brigade said the fire originated in the roof, not the operating box, and the most likely cause was wiring.

The most unfortunate part of the fire was that although the building itself was insured, the fittings and the seats were not. About 610 seats, valued at £2,000, would have to be replaced. The proprietor, Mr H. Kessler Howes, had to bear this loss, and because of this the cinema never opened again.

Later the building was used for indoor golf, then as a fund-collecting centre for Southend hospital. In February 1929 it was being used as a soup kitchen. During November 1931 two local businessmen were interested in converting the Theatre De Luxe into a modern theatre for the presentation of repertory, but the scheme never got off the ground.

The building was finally demolished in May 1936, and Dixon's department store was extended over the site.

GAUMONT

Southend

The Hippodrome Theatre was built on the site of 2/4 Southchurch Road, at a cost of £20,000, and opened on 8 November 1909. As one of Southend's most notable buildings, it was constructed in the English Renaissance style from the designs of Bertie Crewe. The Hippodrome had seating accommodation for 1,750 patrons, and was part of the De Frece theatre circuit, the variety programmes being equal to the best in the provinces.

There were two performances nightly at 6.50 p.m. and 9 p.m. Admission prices were 3d., 6d., 9d., 1/- and 1/6d. Boxes 10/6d. and 15/-. The advertisements proclaimed: 'Always a star programme, two hours of bright varieties.'

Crowds flocked to see all the big names of the variety theatre – Marie Lloyd, George Robey, Houdini, Florrie Ford, Little Tich, Flanagan and Allen and Gracie Fields in her clogs and shawl, all appeared at the Hippodrome.

Through the amalgamation of circuits, the Hippodrome became part of the General Theatre Corporation (G.T.C.) in March 1928. This was taken over by the Gaumont British Picture Corporation in May 1928.

On Saturday 15 August 1930, a huge crowd saw the crowning of Southend's Carnival Queen; there was standing room only in all parts of the house. During April 1933 the Hippodrome began presenting a mixture of cine-variety.

On 6 January 1934 the Hippodrome Theatre closed; the last show was 'Lord John Sangers 1934 Circus Sensation'. Work had already commenced on transforming the theatre into the Gaumont Palace cinema. This did not only consist of a mere change of name, but radical alterations to the building itself; even the pavement outside was re-laid. A magnificent new canopy was erected, bearing the name of the film showing that week. The façade was decorated with neon lighting, and the name of the cinema in electric lights. The front of the building was raised to accommodate a new projection box, which was built on the roof, the projection ports being cut in the ceiling at the rear of the gallery. Often the conversion of theatres into cinemas was not without its problems, especially where projection was concerned. The alterations at the Gaumont resulted in a very steep throw. To compensate for this, the screen (which was the latest type, made of perforated rubber) had to be fitted at an angle, which made the viewing from the front stalls difficult and slightly distorted. Often sightlines in theatres converted to cinemas were poor.

Inside a new lighting system had been arranged, which looked very effective. High against the ceiling were coloured electric 'ceiling roses'. The main colour scheme was extremely beautiful, being in delicate shades of pink and green. The walls were decorated in 'plasticpaint' and coloured silver and gold. The orchestra pit had been removed, giving a larger space to the front stalls. In the top gallery the forms from its theatre days still remained.

The seating had been rearranged to provide more room and comfort, with seating capacity reduced to 1,588. In the theatre days there had been four boxes, two each side of the stage. After alterations only the lower one on each side remained, the others having been replaced by silk covered grilles, which were flood-lit from behind. A British Acoustic sound system had been installed, and, in order to ensure that the sound was equally distributed all over the building, two mighty speakers were installed, instead of the usual one. The top one of these speakers was tilted slightly, so that the sound could be heard plainly in the circle and gallery. Also the management tried as far as possible to re-engage the former members of staff.

The Gaumont Palace cinema opened on 15 January 1934 as part of the Gaumont British circuit. The opening ceremony was performed by the Mayor, Councillor H.F. Frith, who, after a short address, declared the building open and expressed the hope that success would

16   *The Gaumont Palace on opening day.*

17   *A children's matinée at the Gaumont in 1937.*

attend the efforts of the British Gaumont company. The opening films were Clifford Mollison and Constance Shotter in *Meet My Sister*, supported by Tom Walls and Ralph Lynn in *A Cuckoo in the Nest*.

On 19 December 1935 a special performance at the Gaumont Palace was packed from floor to ceiling with hundreds of children drawn from various homes in the borough. For many weeks the cinema had been collecting donations from their patrons, who had given generously. At the end of the performance every child was given a bag containing toys, sweets and fruit. A Mickey Mouse and a cowboy film had delighted the children. The show was arranged by Mr Moneypenny, the cinema's manager.

Mrs E. Raven recalls:

In 1936, my husband's (Frederick Francis Raven), first job at leaving school was to be page boy at the Gaumont. He was uniformed like a commissionaire, with peaked hat and braid, and complete with buttons all down his chest, which had to be cleaned regularly. His greatest thrill was to present a bouquet of flowers to his idol of the screen at that time Margaret Lockwood. One of his sadder memories, more disappointment in his fellow man, was when he found a lady's bag, containing two hundred pounds. He ran after her as she got into her limousine, and she did not even thank him, but he still felt he had done his duty as a good page of the cinema.

The picture house was renamed just 'Gaumont' in 1937. On 1 July 1946 queues outside the cinema were rewarded by the arrival of film star Valerie Hobson, prior to her making

18   *Interior of the Gaumont, 1946.*

a personal appearance on the stage. The star's visit was in conjunction with the pre-release showing of *The Years Between*, in which she starred with Michael Redgrave. Audiences at the Gaumont had met Miss Hobson before, when in 1938 she had selected the Carnival Queen for that year, Miss Margot Sewill. Mr J. Smith, Divisional Publicity manager, introduced Miss Hobson to the audience, whilst a bouquet of roses was presented to the star by five-year-old Vivienne Munds of Christchurch Road, a member of the Gaumont British Junior Club. Tall, slim and attractive, Miss Hobson was very warmly received by the full house and won her audience by her charm and unassuming manner.

The cinema came under the control of J. Arthur Rank with the merger of Gaumont with the Odeon circuit in 1948. In January 1954 the previous attendance record at the cinema was beaten by 3,000, when 22,000 people, in the space of seven days, saw the Norman Wisdom film *Trouble In Store*. Seating capacity of the Gaumont at that time was 1,500, and the staff worked miracles to achieve this record. Crowds queued for an hour before performances and staff gave up their tea breaks.

On 11 February 1954 the film being presented was *Hell Below Zero*, but it was somewhat hotter inside the Gaumont due to a blaze! Miss Rene Monk, the second operator at the cinema, was first to give warning. Shortly before opening she smelt smoke and immediately told the manager Mr William Wood. Although midday, Southend Fire Brigade arrived within a minute of Mr Wood's telephone call. Firemen fought their way through blinding smoke and fumes to a fire raging beneath the stage. The blaze was pin-pointed to a store directly beneath the stage. While hacking through to the basement with axes, part of the stage collapsed, taking one of the firemen with it. He was quickly hauled out, shaken but unharmed. Police using loudspeakers diverted traffic and kept the lunch-time crowd on the move. The Strand cinema, adjoining the Gaumont, did not open until 2 p.m. on the advice of the police. Clouds of thick black smoke billowed from the building into the street, which rapidly became a bustle of firemen, wriggling hoses and cinema usherettes hurrying to and fro with pots of tea. In the midst of this activity stood an elderly lady, patiently waiting. The chief operator asked her what she wanted and she replied, 'What time do you open?'

Thousands of gallons of water were poured into the rear end of the building, and after two hours the fire was brought under control. Barely had the Fire Brigade finished work on the charred mass, which had once been a stage, than more than 50 workmen moved in to carry out repairs. They worked through the night and next morning, making it possible for the Gaumont to be reopened for business at five o'clock on the Friday, just over 24 hours after the blaze. Technicians from London worked side by side with the cinema staff to install a new battery of speakers, erect a new screen and repair the stage. As work progressed, so cleaners followed in their wake clearing up the mess. As the cinema reopened, hundreds queued to see the film starring Alan Ladd.

In August 1954 the cinema was completely redecorated, and the last areas of damage caused by the fire repaired, so wiping away the last traces of the fire. Also a Cinemascope screen was installed ready for the first presentation in this process.

With falling admissions, the Rank Organisation did not need three cinemas in the town, and the Gaumont was by far the oldest building. The cinema closed on 12 October 1956 with the film *A Hill In Korea*, starring Stanley Baker, supported by Kenneth More in *Raising A Riot*.

There was local demand from residents and historical groups to save the building and turn it into a community centre. The council refused, mainly because Rank wanted £50,000, plus a restriction against the building being used as a cinema, ballroom or dance school. It was subsequently sold and the building was demolished in 1958. A supermarket was built on the site, which has since been various retail stores over the years.

19 *Fire at the Gaumont!*

GARONS

Southend

On 28 October 1910, local businessman, Harry Garon, announced his plans to build a picture palace and café in the Broadway (now called the High Street), on the site of Nelson's China Stores, facing Warrior Square. The announcement immediately caused widespread interest. Mr Garon stated that the building would have a frontage of 75 feet and a depth of 175 feet. The picture palace would also be luxuriously furnished, have a proscenium width of 30 feet, and provide seating for 600 patrons. The architect was Bertie Crewe, who had designed the Southend Hippodrome and nearly 70 similar places of entertainment throughout England.

By January 1911 the construction had commenced. Garons Imperial Bioscope was built at a cost of £5,000 and opened on 27 July 1911. The panelled walls of the auditorium were painted white. Subdued top lighting had been introduced, and the floor was carpeted. The advertisements stated: 'The Bioscope sheet is 18 feet square and the auditorium fireproof. A vacuum cleaner will be used daily to ensure perfect sanitation'. The café area provided seating for 300 patrons. Mr J.C. Flaxman, of Southchurch Road, had been in charge of the contract.

There was a large gathering of representative townspeople at the opening ceremony which had been timed for 3.15 p.m. By that hour most of the well-known people of the Borough, and members of the Town Council and the Magistracy, occupied the comfortable armchairs of the auditorium. Councillor H. Garon, managing director of the Bioscope, received the Mayor, Ald. J.C. Ingram, and welcomed him to the cinema. The Mayor stated that they had assembled there that afternoon to add another link to the progress and prosperity of the Borough. In past years they had known what it was to have poverty in the town, but he could truthfully say that no man had done more to help the poor and deserving than Harry Garon. Concluding, the Mayor said the remainder of his task was very simple, and that was to declare the hall open for the public, and he sincerely hoped the whole venture would prove the success it deserved, and the character of the picture show would be an uplift to those who visited it.

Mrs Garon then handed the Mayor a specially wrought spanner of silver, with which her husband asked him to affix, at the opposite end of the hall, a tablet commemorating

20 *Garons Imperial Bioscope in 1911.*

the event. The Mayor then went to the rear of the hall and secured the plaque, which was inscribed, 'Imperial Bioscope Theatre. This tablet was affixed in commemoration of the opening day by Ald. James Colbert Ingram. 27 May 1911. Architect Bertie Crewe, London. Builders J.C. Flaxman, Southend'. The Mayor then proceeded to cause the commencement of the opening programme and, as the portrait of King George V appeared on the screen, members of the Choral Society led the National Anthem. Subsequently the Carlyle Ladies Orchestra, who had been specially engaged for the performance, played selections during a programme of various types of short films. Afterwards light refreshments were dispensed in the café. Garons Imperial Bioscope was to become one of Southend's most successful and best loved cinemas.

After the sudden demise of Harry Garon (not long after the opening of the Bioscope), Garons commercial empire was managed by his son Harry Frank Garon. On 22 March 1912 Harry F. Garon announced that he had secured the sole rights for the district of the famous Kinemacolor process and would revive the showing of Kinemacolor films in the town (they had previously been shown at the Kinemacolor Theatre, in Warrior Square). A couple of weeks later coloured pictures of King George V visiting India were shown.

The *Southend Graphic* reported:

Kinemacolor – The last word in colour pictures, is being shown at the Imperial Bioscope Theatre, and its success has been complete and immediate. Never before has it been shown with such effect in the borough as at this palatial picture palace. The effect is magical and realistic in the extreme, bringing scenes before the spectator, with life-like fidelity.

Harry F. Garon stated:

The installation of the Kinemacolor has entailed considerable expense and trouble. But the arrangements are now complete, and patrons of the Imperial Bioscope will be in a position of seeing these world-renowned pictures amid sumptuous and comfortable surroundings. Music will be rendered by the Bijou Orchestra.

Much anxiety was caused to the staff and management of the Imperial Bioscope on 30 August 1912 when a change of motor generators took place, but by the third day of operation the excellence of the new power had given great satisfaction to both staff and patrons of the cinema.

A two-manual Estey organ was installed in 1921; it was mounted below stage level and was not on a lift. This instrument was played by local ladies, Miss Ena Baga and her sisters Celesta and Florence; the latter had married band leader Harry de Jong. This organ was removed to St Luke's Church, Southend, in 1927. The replacement organ was a two-manual Christie, inaugurated by Nelson Elms, who later went to Blackpool. Rita Legget and her trio played in the adjacent café for afternoon teas. During 1920, a fine ballroom was added above the cinema, and the picture house was renamed simply Garons Cinema.

21   *The auditorium of the Imperial Bioscope in 1911.*

22 *Garons cinema in 1928.*

In 1929, the picture house underwent alterations, with the auditorium being extended, which increased the seating capacity to 916. Also the equipment was installed for sound films. The first film was *The Wolf of Wall Street*, starring George Bancroft and Nancy Carroll, which was screened on 14 October 1929. Garons was only beaten by seven days to being the first cinema in the town to show talkies (the Rivoli's first sound film was shown on 7 October).

Mr J.H. Radford, who worked at Garons, recalls a typical week's work in those days would be something like 70 hours for £2 3s. 6d. In 1935, equipment was installed to change the cinema from D.C. to A.C. current. Also improvements were made to the stage and decorative lighting.

Throughout intermissions, at each side of the screen, fountains would send up jets of water about three feet high, while being illuminated by coloured lights. These survived until 1956 when a wider screen was installed, leaving only about six inches of stage at each side, and no more room for one of the cinemas last links with the past. The Christie organ had been removed to St Stephen's Church, Prittlewell, the previous year.

23   *Interior of Garons cinema, 1928.*

The only reminder of the bygone days was the admission prices, which were still only 10d. during the war, rising to 1/- in 1945, and remaining at this price, until increasing to 1/6d. (after 3.30 p.m. and only for adults), shortly before the cinema's closure on 4 May 1963. The last films were: *Atlantis, The Lost Continent*, starring Anthony Hall and Joyce Taylor, supported by Clark Gable and Sophia Loren in *It Started In Naples*. The manager at that time was Mr H.W. Lake, who had been appointed to that post in 1955, but had actually joined the cinema in 1941, as projection box boy. It is interesting to note that Garons cinema was never converted for 'Cinemascope' presentations.

The building was very promptly demolished and shops and offices were built on the site.

GEM

Southend

On 11 October 1910 plans were submitted to the building inspector's office for the erection of the Gem Electric Theatre, at 6 Victoria Avenue (Victoria Circus), Southend. This was for the conversion of a former garage building into the cinematograph theatre. The owner was Mr F.F. Ramuz, of 8 San Remo Parade, Westcliff.

The seating area of the cinema would be on a single floor. On the building's frontage, the pay box and operating room would partly project out into a tar paved area. The plans were approved on 9 November 1910.

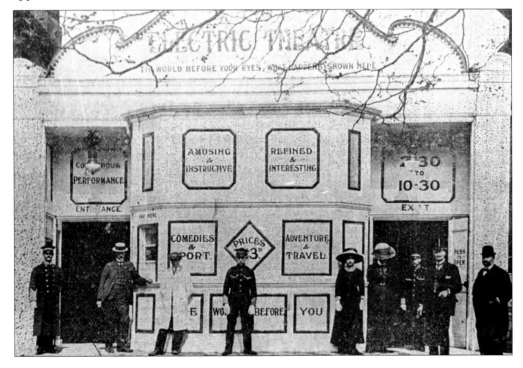

24   *The Gem Electric Theatre, 1913.*

1911 was to prove to be one of the best years for Southend's film enthusiasts, with no fewer than three picture houses opening in the borough. The Gem Electric Theatre opened in May 1911. Performances were continuous between 2.30 p.m. and 10.30 p.m. Admission charges were 2d. and 3d.

The cinema's fascia was covered with various inscriptions such as: 'The World Before Your Eyes', 'What Happens Shown Here' and 'Amusing, Instructive, Refined and Interesting, The World Before You'.

The Gem Electric Theatre enjoyed only a short life; it closed in 1922, and became the Gem Bazaar. The building was demolished in the mid-'20s to make way for the Victoria Arcade complex. The site has more recently been redeveloped into the Hammerson shopping centre, now the Victoria Plaza.

STRAND

Southend

The year 1911 saw the opening of another very successful cinema and one which was to have a colourful life. The building had been erected in Warrior Square as a skating rink, and opened on 15 October 1909 as 'The Rinkeries'. During September 1911 plans were deposited with the planning department for an operator's box and generating room by Kinemacolor Concessions Ltd. These were approved, and the building was converted into a cinema, opening as the Kinemacolor Theatre on 14 October 1911.

With a seating capacity of 1,000 on a single level, the cinema was very commodious, well heated and comfortable, and had the distinction of showing these early colour films, introduced to local audiences by Mr A. Simpson, of Kensington Road, Southend. They had an immediate impact on audiences. Local newspaper reports stated: 'Kinemacolor is amazing! Of all the Metropolitan novelties which have been introduced to this town, few have achieved the instantaneous success of Kinemacolor. The only stereoscopic life motion pictures, in the actual colours of nature, without the aid of artificial tinting. It is the latest sensation in the picture world to be introduced to Southend. Kinemacolor is the greatest advance in the science and art of portraying and exhibiting animated pictures in natural colour. This unique entertainment cannot be seen at any other picture theatre in Essex.' Prices of admission ranged from 1/- to 3d. Performances were twice daily at 3 p.m. and 7 p.m., and afternoon teas were a speciality.

On 17 May 1912 the cinema became the Warrior Square Picture Theatre. The manager was Douglas Ware. During July 1912 an electric plant was installed which pumped 4,000,000 cubic feet of fresh air per hour into the theatre. Admission prices were 3d. and 2d., and performances were continuous between 6 p.m. and 10.30 p.m., with matinées at 2.30 p.m. on Wednesday and Saturday.

On 11 September 1919 the cinema was renamed the Strand, and the ownership changed to Mr Frank Baker. A magnificent pipe organ was installed, at a cost of £4,000. The advertisements proudly proclaimed the Strand as being, 'The Home of the Pipe Organ'. This instrument had been supplied by William Hill and Son, of London. Solo organist was Florence De Jong (late of the Marble Arch Pavilion). The cinema also boasted a full orchestra (musical director Mr Harry De Jong, former conductor at Sextons West End Cinema). The Strand also held first exhibition rights of all the famous Lasky pictures.

When the Mayor's Unemployment Committee met at the Council Chamber, in Southend, on 6 January 1926, the clerk Mr A. Hutchings reported that the proprietors of the Strand cinema gave tickets to a hundred children of the unemployed, every Saturday morning, and allowed them in free. When they came out each child was given a bag of sweets. Mr Hutchings added, that those who had no tickets were admitted for 2d., and when they came out and were handed their sweets, had asked for their 2d. back!

On Sunday, 14 November 1926 the Strand was completely destroyed by fire. The blaze was discovered at 5.00 a.m., and caused £35,000 damage. By 5.30 a.m. the building was a raging furnace, with flames leaping 40 feet high. The roof slates exploded like rockets, and pieces of blazing wood were carried by the high wind onto the roofs of houses in Southchurch Road. Some blazing debris struck a woman standing in a doorway in Warrior Square, and burnt her badly. There was no hope of saving the cinema. All the fire brigade could do was try to save adjoining properties, which they were successful in doing. People in their night attire flocked from the surrounding streets to see the spectacle.

The only part of the cinema left standing was the box office and projection room, which were situated at the High Street end of the building. One projector was destroyed; the other was damaged, but was repairable. The film was undamaged, being stored in steel boxes. The roof had caved in and the organ melted. The only part of the organ left was the two pedals. £6,000 would not replace this instrument. Forty people including the orchestra were thrown out of work. The cause of the fire was unknown; a cigarette had been discounted as the fire had

25   *The remains of the Strand after the 1926 fire.*

started near the roof. In those days telephones were few, and the owner Mr Frank Baker lived at Leigh, so friends rushed to his house, to tell him the cinema was destroyed. Mr Baker was then driven to Southend, in dressing gown and pyjamas, to behold the tragic sight.

'Billy', the mottled cat who slept and lived on the premises, was missed after the fire, and everyone feared the worst, but, to the astonishment of all, the feline was seen prowling round the debris the next day.

Curiously enough, *Safety First* was the film to be shown that week at the Strand, and the nearby Hippodrome sported vivid posters of firemen and hoses with *False Alarm*, as the attraction for the week.

A number of people still have vivid memories of the Strand fire.

Mr A.L. Foreman recalls:

I was only a small boy when the Stand caught fire, but my father who was a milkman and had to be about at the ungodly time of 5.30 a.m., told me that he saw the flames and heard the wood cracking as he left home. My cousin who was a volunteer fireman and attended the fire, told me of the trials and tribulations he had to endure, trying to get his fire boots, belt and axe back to their pristine glory in time for the Mayors Procession, at 10.30 a.m., on the Sunday morning.

Mrs J. Bousfield remembers:

Before the fire, us children would go to a little church in Clarence Street and queue for a 2d. ticket, then to the Strand and queue to get in for the Saturday morning show. We were given a bag of sweets and an orange for the ticket, and all trooped in to see Jack Holt in *The Flying Squad*. We were very upset to hear the building had caught fire, and my friend and I went to investigate to find if it was true. A fireman took us inside and with his hatchet broke the remainder of the glass on all the chocolate machines, which stood around the edge of the cinema. 1d. Nestles flat bars in red paper, but because of the heat, had melted into different shapes, but was still very edible and thoroughly enjoyed.

A new picture house was built on the site, the general contractor being Arthur J. Arnold. The frontage of the building in Warrior Square was 90 feet wide, the entrance being in modern Renaissance style, with 'Hathernware' Faience tiling, to match the adjoining Strand arcade. The auditorium was 131 feet long and 70 feet wide, with a sloping floor, which had a comfortable rake of seven feet. The proscenium width was 34 feet and the depth of the stage 16 feet. The seating capacity was 1,640, and the walls were finished in cream fibrous plaster, the curtains (by Messrs Kemballs, of Westcliff) and seats were in a restful shade of blue. Heating was achieved by a hot water installation with radiators, while the lighting effects were secured by electricity, with an auxiliary gas-lighting plant in case of a breakdown.

The cinema opened on Saturday, 28 January 1928. A distinguished company gathered for the opening, which was performed by the Mayor, Councillor A. Bockett. The guests included many members of the town council, Mrs Eleanor Percy (chairman of directors of the Warrior Square Picture Theatre Ltd), and Mr Frank Baker (managing director). After Mr Harold Judd had sung 'Land of Hope and Glory', and Mr D.H. Burles (architect), had briefly described the new building, the Mayor was invited formally to declare it open.

26   *The new Strand cinema in 1930.*

The Mayor said that upon arriving outside the Strand he had found a certain apparatus facing him, and he supposed that he would later be shown upon the screen. He objected to that unless he was to receive the same rate of remuneration as Douglas Fairbanks or Charlie Chaplin. He then went on to say, 'Upon the ashes of the old Strand Cinema has risen a theatre of considerable beauty, I congratulate the architects, the builder, and the other contractors who have taken part in the erection of this building, that is an asset to the County Borough.' He then declared the new Strand Cinema open.

Chocolates were distributed to ladies in the audience, and after the screening of 'The Old Strand and the New', the opening film was presented, *Seventh Heaven* starring Janet Gaynor and Charles Farrell.

Although the screen and main entrance were at the Warrior Square end of the building, the cinema had the unusual distinction of having a second entrance at the other end, entry being gained through a tunnel from the High Street. The replacement organ was a three-manual 'Kinora', which many patrons felt produced a rather unpleasant sound when compared with the remarkably fine pipe organ in the old cinema. The new instrument also seemed weak for the size of the building. A good orchestra, however, was retained.

Mrs J. Bousfield says of the new building:

The cinema had been rebuilt without the little wall across the front. People waiting to gain entry from the High Street, would queue along the tunnel between the shops, and would often get mixed in the with the Gaumont queue which would stretch along Leather Lane to the Strand. Sometimes a talent competition was held on a Friday night. Our neighbour used to volunteer for a small box of chocolates. Also a little prize was given for anyone who had anything unusual in their pockets or bag, like a chisel, screwdriver or such.

A Western Electric sound system was installed for the 'talkies', which was changed in April 1934 for Western Electric Wide Range sound equipment. On 7 March 1937 the cinema was sold by Mr Frank Baker to Messrs Mistlin Theatres Ltd, who were building up a new circuit. The directors of the company were David and Louis Mistlin, the latter becoming manager of the Strand.

During August 1940 the Strand devised a scheme for helping patrons to assist the war effort. Special boxes were provided by the management, so old keys could be collected for making guns and shells. The cinema set the million mark as its aim, and with the help of every patron this was accomplished in a short time. By the late '40s the seating capacity of the Strand had been reduced to 1,550.

On 15 June 1955 the cinema was taken over by the Essoldo circuit, and took on a new lease of life. It was Essoldo's fifth cinema in the area, having the year before taken over the Metropole and Mascot at Westcliff, and the Corona and Coliseum at Leigh.

The Essoldo circuit was formed by northern entrepreneur Solly Sheckman, who in 1930 purchased two cinemas in the North East, and by adding further halls, formed North East

27   *The Essoldo a few days after closing in 1960.*

28   *Interior of the Essoldo just after closure.*

Coast Cinemas. The circuit expanded during the war and the 'Essoldo' name was created out of the names Esther, Solly and Dorothy Sheckman (Esther was Solly's wife and Dorothy his daughter). During the 'fifties' the Essoldo circuit had grown to almost two hundred cinemas, and was thought of as 'the third circuit', the two majors being A.B.C. and a combined Gaumont/Odeon under Rank control.

Immediately work began on the Strand. A 47-feet-wide Mural Mirror Cinemascope screen was installed, together with four-channel, magnetic, stereophonic sound equipment. The Essoldo was the only town-centre cinema to have this new sound system. The proscenium had also been modernised and widened to take the new screen.

On 19 June 1955 the cinema presented the Cinemascope film *Untamed*, starring Tyrone Power and Susan Haywood. At that time the American 20th Century Fox films were released through the Essoldo and Granada circuits, providing these cinemas with a lot of excellent films to present. The Strand was renamed Essoldo on 20 November 1955. Mr Louis Carr was manager, and Mrs Iris Avery assistant manager.

Mr A.L. Foreman was a member of the Southend Fire Brigade fire prevention department, and has the following memories of the Essoldo:

> In August, 1955, the brigade was called when one of the electric motors driving the ventilator fans, overheated in the ceiling and sparks drifted down on the audience. With the exception of one man, the people chose to ignore them. This one man leapt to his feet and started to shout, only to be told to stop shouting by Mr Carr, and asked to resume his seat. The fan was shut

off, cooled down and checked by the Brigade, and then the programme continued without a hitch. On the second occasion, the brigade was called to the cinema to release a young male attendant who had got himself trapped under the timber members supporting the organ pipes. Apparently this lad had crawled under the structure in search of the cinema cat. Anyway, when we arrived we were conducted to the roof space by the same manager, Mr Carr. It appeared that due to the layout of the timber members, the only way we could get to this lad was by dismantling the pipes and go in at the top, to which the manager gave his consent. 'Bloody thing is never used anyway' was his comment. I was a bit narrower in the waist then than I am now and I found that by removing my belt and tunic I could squeeze in between the uprights, and get down to the lad. I found that his shoulders were wedged under the timber beam, but when I tried to ease him back he hollered that his arm was down a hole. After much heaving and shoving I found that his arm was doubled under his body and had apparently gone numb. I called for a jack and handle, got this under the member and after some very expensive sounding creaks and cracks, levered the member up a few inches, enough to give me room to move him back a bit so the rest of the crew could reach through and grab his feet, and pull him out, ignoring his yells about his arm being down a hole. Other than being frightened out of his wits he was okay, but I believe they took him to hospital to be on the safe side. While we were attending to him, the cat strolled out quite unconcerned.

The Essoldo ownership was to prove somewhat brief, the cinema closing on Saturday, 14 May 1960. The last films were *Doctor At Large* starring Dirk Bogarde, and Norman Wisdom in *Man of the Moment*. The cinema was still making money, but was a victim of big business. The building had been purchased by Keddies Stores for £35,000. The cinema was gutted and fitted out as Supa-Save, one of Southend's first supermarkets. Later the building was demolished and Keddies store was extended over the site.

An advertisement from the days of the panoramic screen installation was still in the windows over the High Street, long after the cinema had disappeared. It proclaimed: 'See our new Cinemascope screen, viewed without the aid of glasses'. The old cinema entrance tunnel between the High Street shops also remained for quite a number of years.

29 *Essoldo monthly film programme booklet.*

REGAL

Southend

During May 1919 plans were deposited with the building inspector's office for the Arcadia Theatre. These plans were later greatly modified, and then approved by the council on 17 June 1919. The theatre was built in Tylers Avenue, next to the fire station. The owner was Mr Herman Darewski, and the architects Burles & Harris, of Southend. The theatre opened on 16 August 1920 with a variety show; top of the bill was popular tenor John Luxton.

In August 1921 the building came under the management of Mr Herbert Jay, who was well-known for his various interests in the theatrical world. Mr Jay was not only connected with the Kingsway and Ambassadors' theatres in London, but also with provincial theatres and touring companies.

In October 1921 the Arcadia closed, and under the direction of Mr F.G. Bethley, of Westcliff, the building was renovated and re-decorated, reopening on 27 February 1922 as the Ambassadors' Theatre. The opening play was 'The French Dancer', with Jane Wood. Prices of admission were Orchestra Stalls 3/6d., Pit Stalls 2/4d. and Pit 1/3d. Programmes changed weekly, and were performed by various companies. There was one presentation each evening at 8 p.m., and a matinée on Wednesday afternoons.

The seating capacity of the Ambassadors' theatre was 800, on a single floor. The seats were plush covered and constructed on the tip-up principle. Each side of the auditorium, separated from the main body of the hall by a low balustrade, were lounges, connected by a promenade at the rear of the hall, where patrons could take tea during the performance. The stage had been widened, with the dressing rooms and other accommodation for the players situated on each side. The building was heated throughout by radiators and excellently ventilated. The dignified colour scheme consisted of a ground-work of pink, with inset tapestry gilt panels. There was a marked absence of the lavish gilding which adorned so many places of entertainment. There were three entrances, the two at either extremity of the building's frontage having box offices, while above were the managerial rooms.

30   *The interior of the Ambassadors' Theatre, 1926.*

In 1923, the lessee of the theatre was Mr H. Hodgson-Bentley, who founded the Southend Repertory Company.

In June, 1929, Mr Hodgson-Bentley stated that the rumours that the theatre was about to close were untrue, although the theatre had suffered a bad season. On 1 August 1930 it was announced that a new share issue of £2,700 had been fully subscribed by the public. The theatre was redecorated to the design of Andrew Mather, the famous theatre designer and decorator, who was responsible for the decoration of many of the most important London theatres. Green, blue and silver were the predominant colours in the Ambassadors'. The front of the theatre was re-seated, and a row of seats in front of the orchestra removed to make a gangway. An orchestra of five had been engaged, who had been playing together for two-and-a-half years, at Boot's café, in the High Street.

With sound films now taking the entertainment scene by storm the Ambassadors' Theatre struggled on for a time, but finally, due to lack of support, it closed on 18 April 1931. The last play was 'The Girl From Upstairs'. The Southend Repertory Company felt they had been carrying on a losing battle for some time. Some of the local amateur dramatic societies hoped that collectively they might be able to save the theatre, but something quite different was about to happen – the building was converted into a cinema.

While conversion work was in progress a young electrician was seriously injured in a very unfortunate accident. The apprentice was working in the roof of the building, assisting with the electrical wiring, when his foot slipped and he fell through the beams in the roof void, dropped to the ceiling about five feet below, and then through the white plaster ceiling to the floor of the auditorium, a further fall of about 28 feet. Fellow workmen rushed to his aid, and he was taken to Victoria Hospital and later Rochford Hospital where he was detained, suffering from severe concussion, cuts to his face and arms, and shock. Fortunately the lad had fallen on the clear space on the floor. Had he fallen on to the seats his injuries would doubtless have been of a far more serious nature.

The building was reopened as the Regal cinema on 1 November 1931. The opening film was *Dirigible*, starring Jack Holt and Fay Wray, supported by *Lover Come Back*, with Betty Bronson. Prices of admission were 1/6d., 1/3d., 1/-, 9d. and 6d. The lessees of the cinema were Southchurch Entertainments Ltd, who also owned the Mascot cinema, Westcliff, and the Plaza, Southchurch.

During the months it had been closed the building had been altered structurally and re-decorated throughout. It was hoped that by the time the alterations were complete the seating capacity would be increased to around 1,000.

Managing director Mr L.H. Jackson had shown praiseworthy local pride in entrusting the decoration of the cinema entirely to local designers and executors. The results were beautiful; the interior of the building was a tribute to the local workmen. The novelty of the decoration, with its panelled eastern scenes, and light and gilded entrance hall was striking. Considering the short time of its closure, the results of the alterations were little short of miraculous.

The projection box had been enlarged, and fitted with new fire shutters, and a new fire exit onto the roof had been built. The exterior of the building had been painted in a cheerful stone colour, and the staff were supplied with brown and silver uniforms. The cinema was successful for five years, but the opening of three large cinemas in the town during 1934-35 (the Gaumont, Ritz and Astoria) made it impossible for the Regal to continue as a cinema, and the picture house closed on 16 November 1935. The last films were *Cavalcade* starring Diana Wynyard and Clive Brook, supported by *Krakatoa*.

The Regal reopened on 26 December 1935, once again as a theatre, presenting variety shows and occasional stage plays. The reopening show was the pantomime 'Aladdin'. Once

31   *The Regal cinema in 1935.*

32 *The Regal Theatre awaiting demolition in 1963.*

again the building had been decorated and re-seated, together with the installation of a new lighting system, and update of the dressing rooms, which included the supply of hot and cold water. Also two large dressing rooms had been built under the stage area. The foyer was now decorated in Nile green and cream. In the auditorium gold and green lanterns had been fitted over the ceiling lights, and the entire floor re-laid in parquet. The resident general manager was Mr P.H. Alexander, who had over 30 years' experience as a stage artiste. The theatre had a full orchestra, under the direction of Mr Charles H. Meek, formerly conductor at the Hippodrome, Southend. By 1941, the Regal was part of the Regis Theatre Group.

On 3 December 1946, approval was sought at Southend Justices Court for plans for proposed alterations at the Regal, to increase the seating capacity by 80 seats, from 756 to 836. This was to enable the management of the theatre to get higher grade touring companies at the theatre. The grading of such companies was governed by the seating capacity of the theatre.

On 16 March 1948 Frank Nash, the Southend United goalkeeper, fainted in the Regal, while watching the show with two other players. He was carried out and given first aid treatment at the fire station, next door. During a practice match in the morning Mr Nash had injured his knee, and it was thought his collapse was a secondary shock.

During the late '40s the variety shows were sometimes mixed with presentations of the 'latest discoveries', the Carroll Levis show being one such production. Nude reviews were also introduced in an effort to boost audiences, and such shows were presented at the Regal well into the '50s. The beautiful Phyllis Dixey was one of the top artistes in these reviews, famous as the girl the Lord Chamberlain banned, following her appearance as 'Eve' in the show 'Eve on Parade'.

By now competition to the theatres was not only coming from cinemas, but also television, which had also started presenting variety shows, so people could sit at home and see all their favourite artistes. The Regal was now struggling to keep going, and losing money. Some of the shows were generally poor, and at the first house there were seldom many patrons. Finally the theatre was put into the hands of liquidators, and on the orders of the receiver the Regal closed on 23 October 1954. The last show was 'Crazy Dames', performed by the Forces Showtime Company.

Once again it was hoped that, if the local amateur societies combined their resources, they might be able to purchase the Regal. But this hope was not realised, and the theatre was sold for around £20,000, and became a warehouse. Finally in August 1963 the Regal was demolished, together with the surrounding buildings, and the site became a car park.

CIVIC NEWS THEATRE

Southend

The Talza Arcade complex had been built in Southchurch Road, opposite the Hippodrome Theatre, during the mid-'20s, and was owned by C.H.J. Talmadge. Incorporated in this shopping complex, above the shops, on the first floor, was the Talza Hall, which had been used for dancing, catering and various other functions. During 1932, an application for a theatre licence was approved by the council, and the Talza Hall Theatre opened on 17 October 1932 with a Vaudeville Show performed by the famous 'Concord Follies'. Variety only lasted a short while; the last show, starring Jock Glen, took place on 19 February 1933. On 27 March 1933 the hall was advertised as the New Repertory Theatre and the first play was 'It Pays To Advertise'.

The theatre was not without its difficulties. There was a problem with viewing the stage because of the flat floor, and the very limited stage area did not help. In 1934 a raked floor was installed. Things improved further when the Little Theatre Company started presenting plays on a weekly basis. The first of these plays was 'Meet the Wife'. The theatre had reopened on 16 April 1934 and was now known as the Talza Theatre.

The repertory theatre lasted for four years. Then the Talza Theatre closed on 9 October 1937; the last show was 'Musical Cheers' starring Tony Williams. The hall was converted into a cinema, reopening on 1 March 1938 as the Civic News Theatre, with a seating capacity of 300. The lessee was News Cinemas (Southend) Ltd, whose managing director was Mr Jackson Hartley.

The following report appeared in the *Southend Times* newspaper:

The Newsreel Theatre has become so integral a part of everyday life that one may, perhaps, wonder why Southend has had to wait so long for such an amenity. However the omission has been made good by Mr Jackson Hartley and his associates, and what was, until recently, the Talza Theatre, has been transformed out of recognition and now presents an ideal setting for its purpose. For the convenience of patrons the seating accommodation has been limited to three hundred, although the capacity of the house is greater. The management appreciated the fact that any show is doubly entertaining when comfort is assured, and this essential is certainly forthcoming. The visitor enters an auditorium of ample dimensions, decorated in a pleasing light green and old gold colour scheme, with concealed lighting high in the sides of the walls, supplemented by wall lights. The red and green armchair seats are extremely comfortable in their upholstery, while perfect projection of the pictures is assured, together with excellent sound reproduction, by the installation of the famous Kalee 8 projecting plant. Perfect acoustics and equally perfect vision, with a continuous supply of pure air and a complete draught-excluding system ensure the further comfort of the visitor. The walls are specially constructed of sound absorbing material. The free cloak room is a welcome innovation, and parallel with the auditorium is the Tudor tea lounge, a delightful retreat which happily avoids the heaviness sometimes associated with 'period' lounges. A further transformation has been applied to the

33   *The Civic News Theatre in 1938.*

entrance hall, which has been enlarged and is open both to Southchurch Road and to the adjacent Talza Arcade. Here the attractive scheme is of black Marblexa, with Staybrite steel fittings, and overhead neon signs. It is the intention of the management to present a change of programme twice weekly (on Sundays and Thursdays). The hours of opening will be 12 noon to 10.45 p.m., Sundays 8.00 to 10.30 p.m. Admission prices are 3d., 6d. and 1/-, with any seat 3d. up to 3.30 p.m. (Saturday excepted). The programmes will include first run Gaumont and Universal newsreels, while important events will be shown at the cinema within a few hours of their happening. In addition, interest films will be shown, such as, 'Secrets of Nature', and travel interest features. Finally cartoons and serials will be part of most programmes, as a main point of attraction.

Included in the new cinema building was a parcel room and, perhaps uniquely, writing room facilities. The Civic News Theatre also had the distinction of making its own local newsreel on 16mm film. This was inserted in the programme between the national newsreels, the home-made newsreel having been filmed around Southend during the previous few days by the Civics' own projection staff. Over to one side of the auditorium, at the front, was an alcove and this provided space for a glass-fronted booth. When the local newsreel was presented (this being silent), one of the projection staff would stand inside the booth with a microphone and, while watching the screen, would speak a commentary to the film. Appropriate music would be added from the projection box by the aid of records. So the audio was completely non-sync to the film's visual sequences. For many years the chief projectionist and assistant manager was Mr Andre Nikola-Smith.

On 1 July 1950 the cinema closed, and after repairs and renovation reopened as the New Vic Cinema on 29 October. This name was chosen because letters on the old neon sign

34   *The newly opened Civic News Theatre.*

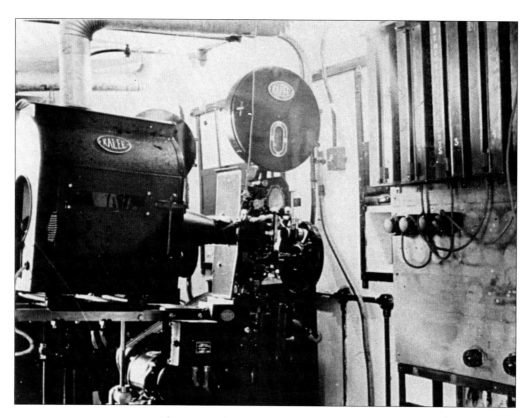

35   *The projection box of the Civic News Theatre in 1938.*

could be rearranged to spell the new name. The seating capacity had now been reduced to 292. It closed again on 9 April 1955 for decoration, and a change of management took place. The cinema reopened on 18 April as the Continental, with a season of foreign films.

The new manager was a young free-lance journalist, Mr George Mann. Mr Mann was a keen filmgoer with extensive experience in cinema management, which he had gained overseas. He also had very definite ideas on the kind of entertainment the public wanted and appreciated, and was confident that in Southend there existed a large audience for Continental films. This proved not to be the case, and the new film booking policy only lasted a short time, the cinema closing again on 12 June 1955. It did not reopen until 19 April 1956, having reverted to the name New Vic, and showing family programmes again. Prices of admission were 1/3d., 1/9d. and 2/3d., all children 1/3d. Every Monday and Thursday all old age-pensioners were admitted at 9d., and received a cup of tea and a biscuit.

Later in the '50s continental films were once again introduced, but the cinema finally closed on 26 September 1959. The last films were Michel Simon in *The Strange Desire of Monsieur Bard* and Pierre Fresnay in *The Aristocrats*. The hall became a strip club, and then a Chinese restaurant. In 1965 the former cinema and the complete arcade complex, together with the whole surrounding area, was demolished to make way for the Hammerson shopping development, now the Victoria Plaza.

RITZ

Southend

Southend's two super cinemas were built in 1935. The first of these was the Ritz, erected on the corner of Grove Road and Church Road, at the top of Pier Hill, near the seafront. The cinema was owned by County Cinemas, designed by Robert Cromie, and built by Messrs. E.D. Winn and Co., of Knightsbridge, in the space of six months by a labour force of four hundred. Three hundred tons of steel was used in the construction of the Ritz. The main elevation, with its varying bands of brick in selected tints, interspersed with stone band courses, was dignified and striking.

On entering the cinema a refreshing note was struck by the restrained and charming effect of the decorative treatment, undertaken by Mollo and Egan, which harmonised with the grouping of the lighting fittings and the fine marble mosaic terrazzo floor. Immediately over the entrance hall was a café, decorated in silver and black, with stately windows which afforded a magnificent view of the seafront. The auditorium revealed an entirely new motif in interior decoration. The main scheme was a comparatively simple one of silver green and gold walls, with luxurious seating in jade green, designed to give maximum comfort and an unimpaired view. The auditorium was 115 feet long and 85 feet wide, and the proscenium opening of 50 feet was the largest in Essex. The exits had been calculated upon the 2,250 seating capacity, and the building could be emptied in two minutes. The modern air conditioning plant was fitted with powerful fans and air washing devices, supplying a continuous flow of pure fresh air into the auditorium. This scientifically treated air was actually purer than the outside atmosphere.

The Conacher organ, a 12-rank, was a very large one. It had the unusual feature of a Grand Piano which was placed on the side of the stage, and could be played by the organist from the organ keyboard. An illuminated casing of beautiful design was fitted around the console, the organist having control of changing colour effects which radiated through the glass. Western Electric Wide Range sound apparatus had been installed together with the latest projectors.

A complicated, but modern electric system had been installed, so arranged that, should the main supply temporarily fail, an alternative and independent supply was immediately

36 *The impressive exterior of the Ritz cinema.*

available. Electricity was the lifeblood of the cinema: it issued tickets, supplied primary, secondary and decorative lighting, stage lighting and control equipment, ventilating motors and air cleaning plant. Electricity supplied the organ equipment and organ lift, projection and sound apparatus, clocks and telephones, and exterior lighting such as floodlighting and neon signs. The total connect electrical load for the Ritz amounted to 250,000 watts, which if used continuously would have consumed 250 units per hour. In practice, as certain equipment was only used during varying intervals of the daily routine, only 1,000 units of electricity was used per day. Safety had been ensured by the fire-resisting qualities of the materials employed, by perfect drainage and fire extinguisher systems. The Ritz was superb, with an imposing frontage, a spacious auditorium, all occupying a commanding site.

The Ritz opened on Thursday, 14 February 1935. Interested crowds had watched the ever-growing queues and the arrival of the guests long before the opening hour. The opening ceremony was performed by the Mayor, Councillor A.T. Edwards, in the presence of a large gathering of representatives of all branches of activity in the life of the Borough. To the cheers of a mighty audience, the handsome fluted stage curtains, rendered lovelier by ever changing lights, parted to reveal the Mayoral party and the trumpeters of H.M. Coldstream

Guards. Then came a fanfare, and the house rose to sing the National Anthem, to the combined accompaniment of the Coldstream Guards Band and the organ, played by Mr Quentin MacLean.

The Mayor advanced to the footlights and complimented the management on their superhuman efforts. He said the building was a wonderful achievement, and it had been marvellous that all concerned had been able to complete the work in readiness for this red-letter date in Southend's entertainment history. The cinema was a valuable addition to the amenities of the town. The Mayor then extended a hearty Southend welcome to the directors of County Cinemas, and said he had much pleasure in declaring the Ritz cinema open.

Then followed a sample of the screen entertainment, consisting of the Gaumont British News, and a 'Silly Symphony'. After which the Ritz super organ rose into view, played by Quentin MacLean, who must have been gratified by the hailstorm of applause which greeted his efforts. Finally the organ, looking like a huge butterfly with multi-coloured wings, disappeared, and the screen entertainment continued with the film *Nell Gwyn*, starring Anna Neagle and Sir Cedric Hardwicke. At the conclusion of the picture, a spotlight fell on the stage and Anna Neagle appeared in person. The evening concluded with a reception in the café.

The film *Nell Gwyn* continued for the week, supported by Richard Bird in *What Happened Then*. Douglas Reeve, the 16-year-old wonder boy organist, in the Eton collar, was appointed to the Ritz, as resident organist. Manager of the Ritz was Mr L. Morley Clarke, who was

37   The Ritz pictured on opening day, 1935.

formerly with the Gaumont British Corporation. Guest organists at the Ritz during the first couple of years included Andrew Fenner, W. Steff-Langston and Guy Hindell.

On 15 June 1935 children's Saturday morning picture shows were commenced, with the grand gala opening of the Mickey Mouse Club. In 1937, the Ritz had a 'Birthday Ball', comprising of dancing 8.30 to 11 p.m. at the *Palace Hotel*. Then at the cinema a midnight matinée was presented of the new British film *Keep Your Seats Please*. Dancing continued again at the Palace until 2.30 a.m. Tickets were 5/-, or 7/6d., including breakfast.

County Cinemas were merged into Oscar Deutsch's Odeon circuit in 1939, which was taken over in June 1940 by J. Arthur Rank, on the tragic early demise of Oscar Deutsch. Because of the wartime conditions the Ritz closed in September 1940, and did not reopen until May 1942. Also the Saturday morning Boys and Girls Club did not reopen until 26 July 1945.

When the Gaumont closed in 1956, the Ritz was redecorated, fitted with new carpet and seating (which was reduced to 1,891), and geared up to become the replacement picture house. A new canopy was fitted to the front of the building, and queuing in the rain was a thing of the past, as the seating capacity of the Ritz could absorb nearly twice the number that could be seated at the Gaumont. Even if all seats were filled, patrons could be accommodated in the warmth of the Ritz's extensive foyer areas. Many of the Gaumont staff transferred to the Ritz, and the picture house would once again become a first-run

38   *The café of the Ritz cinema in 1935.*

39 *Douglas Reeve at the Conacher organ.*

cinema, taking the Gaumont's National release films. Later the café became a ballroom, then subsequently became disused. The organ was removed and went to the Odeon, Blackpool.

A strange incident occurred in September 1956, when a local man was found sitting naked in the balcony of the Ritz. When he later appeared at Southend court, the man pleaded guilty to breaking and entering, but was unable to account for his actions. The judge stated: 'I'm told the cinema has a peculiar effect on some people. It's the first case I have heard of people taking their clothes off, however.'

In 1968, the building received a further facelift, at a cost of £6,000. In a 12-week run 84,000 people saw the film *The Sound of Music*. The Ritz closed for film entertainment on 8 March 1972, the last programme being a John Wayne double bill of *True Grit* and *El Dorado*. Mr Chris Moore of Rank Leisure Services said: 'We are always sorry to lose a cinema, but we have already put one in its place with the new Odeon. The Ritz has steadily been losing money since the twin Odeon cinemas opened. Where cinemas don't pay Bingo seems to be the answer.'

So, at a cost of £100,000 the Ritz was converted into the Top Rank Bingo Club, later being leased out to Invicta bingo. Then the building was closed during 1978, and became derelict. Finally, amid a great outcry from conservationists, and theatre and film enthusiasts, the Ritz was demolished in January 1981. It was described at the time as 'One of the greatest acts of unthinkable destruction Southend has ever known'. The car park of the Royals shopping development is built on the site of the Ritz.

ODEON

Southend

Built on the site of Lukers brewery, at 127 High Street, the Astoria was one of the largest cinemas in the United Kingdom, and certainly Southend's largest and most lavish cinema. It had been announced during February 1929 that Lukers brewery was to go, and work would start shortly on shops and a cinema. The architects were E.A. Stone & T.R. Somerford. Interior decoration was by Mollo & Egan, and the cinema was owned by Astoria Cinemas Ltd.

For months residents of the Borough and thousands of visitors had passed down the High Street and paused to admire the simple but classical lines of the entrance, and many had tried to peep through the hoardings to see what was being prepared for their approval. The site and the building had cost a total of £250,000.

The main elevation of the building was faced with polished biscuit-coloured artificial stone and the window frames were metal. The bronze and green canopy formed a basis for the vertical floodlighting. Coloured tubular lighting outlined the canopy, windows, name sign and its surrounding panel, and also the whole of the upper façade, including the vertical lines of the central section.

Inside the vast foyer, the lofty ceiling and modern 'well' from the tea lounge above gave a truly noble air, which was intensified by the sweeping staircases on either side, and the central low flight of stairs to the stalls. The entrance hall and staircase walls were decorated in a neutral tint of sprayed plastic paint, relieved with gold speckling. Flat lighting panels were flush with the surface of the wall pilasters. The fluting in the ceiling was coloured a trifle darker than the walls. Carpets were black, blue and green.

To one entering the auditorium from the spacious crush hall the spaciousness was striking. The use of lofty columns and a tiered ceiling added to the height of the building.

The auditorium walls were decorated warm pink, shaded with bronze. There was not a visible light source in the whole of the auditorium. The tabs were pale pink and seats blue. A layer of patent asbestos one inch thick had been applied to the rear walls

40   *The opening of the Astoria in 1935.*

of the auditorium, the balcony front and the front of the projection box for acoustical reasons. The side walls were also treated with this material in panel form, the whole being sprayed with a textural paint. The seating capacity was 2,750: 1,750 in the stalls and 1,000 in the balcony. Upstairs wide corridors led to the balcony and tea lounge, the walls of which were treated in a kind of plant motif in black-blue, blues and bronzes. The Astoria was admired for the design as a building of imposing beauty. Avoiding the ornate, the lines of the structure were graceful and its colour schemes tasteful.

Over 2,000,000 bricks were used in the construction of the cinema, and 1,000 tons of steel girders. The electrically-operated safety curtain, one of the largest of its kind, weighed 11.5 tons, and was 58 feet wide by 33 feet high. The stage was one of the four largest in the country, with an opening of 56 feet by 30 feet. When the orchestra pit was brought up to the level of the stage an extra 13 feet of 'apron' was added. The full width of the stage was 120 feet, with 40 feet depth. There were 16 dressing rooms for the artistes, and two large ones for the choruses.

Torches were not necessary for the attendants, as the end seats at each gangway had concealed lighting for the steps. There was no standing room at the back of the auditorium, but there were side promenades where people could wait, and through which they could pass to get to the front part of the house. The projection box had two projectors, four spotlights and an effects lantern.

That the new cinema had captured the imagination of Southenders had long been evident. The culminating point was reached on opening day, 15 July 1935, when a queue for the premiere began to form early in the afternoon and soon reached huge dimensions. At the premiere show, the Astoria was officially opened by the Mayor of Southend, Councillor A.T. Edwards, who was greeted by some 3,000 people. He reminded the audience that as recently as the previous November the site of the theatre had been vacant ground. He was particularly gratified to know that 90 per cent of the labour employed had been local, that the theatre would give regular employment to a hundred persons, and that the orchestra would be a permanent feature of the programmes. The mayor then declared the cinema open to the public.

The opening programme was hailed as the greatest show in Southend's history, the main feature was *Brewsters Millions*, starring Jack Buchanan, and was supported by Gene Raymond, Henry Hull and Francis Drake in *False Witness*. On the stage Francis A. Mangan presented 'The Black Swan', with Doris Niles, the St Hellier Sisters, The Mangan Ensemble and The Corps De Ballet. In addition, on the screen were a 'Silly Symphony', British Movietone News and the Gaumont British Magazine. To complete the programme there

41   *The auditorium of the Astoria on opening day.*

was The Astoria Grand Orchestra, under the direction of Jan Godowsky, and Guy Hindel at the mighty Compton organ. To round off the evening Major C.H. Bell, the managing director, introduced the Astoria personnel. As the curtain rose a realistic representation of Southend pier in centenary garb was revealed, and he presented the front of house staff and Mr Billy Stewart, the manager, to the audience.

After the performance a reception was held in the foyer and café, terminating shortly after midnight. Commencing the following day programmes were continuous daily 12.30 till 11 p.m., Sunday 8 till 10.30 p.m. Admission prices were 9d., 1/-, 1/6d., 2/- and 2/6d.

In June 1936 the Astoria was taken over by County cinemas. When Miss Francis Haywood was crowned as Southend Carnival Queen in August 1936 at the Astoria, American film star Edward G. Robinson made a personal appearance at the ceremony. On 12 May 1937 the Coronation broadcast was relayed direct to the Astoria at 10 a.m., with all admission charges going to charity.

On 20 April 1938 the *Southend Times* reported:

Cinema Operators Go On Strike. There was a break of about twenty minutes in the evening performance at the Astoria cinema on Easter Monday, when without warning, the operators decided to strike in sympathy with the London cinema operators, who came out over the Easter holidays. The interval occurred halfway through the second feature, but deputy operators were found, and the show continued. During the interval, Mr Jack Courtnay, gave a selection of popular songs on the organ. Informed there was a technical hitch, the audience were quite unaffected by the occurrence. Operators were brought down from London the following day, and performances are continuing as usual.

43   *The magnificent Odeon auditorium in 1964.*

County Cinemas was merged with Oscar Deutsch's Odeon circuit in 1939. The ownership of the Odeon circuit passed to J. Arthur Rank after the early demise of Oscar Deutsch, and in June 1940 the cinema was renamed Odeon.

On the evening of 18 January 1944 an incident occurred at the Odeon's pay box. Mrs D. Phillips, the cashier, heard a man's voice from outside the blacked-out pay box demand, 'Give me the cash'. She refused and pressed the alarm buzzer. Twice more the voice gruffly ordered her to hand over the money and, when she still refused, a glass phial of evil-smelling fluid – similar to a schoolboys 'stink bomb' – was thrown through the aperture of the window into the pay box. The man, who could not be seen in the darkness, made off as the commissionaire approached.

During Christmas Day 1944 two boys aged 14 and 16 years robbed a bomb-damaged shop in Westcliff, of nine rounds of rifle ammunition. They then extracted the cordite from the ammunition. Later the same day they took the cordite into the toilets of the Odeon cinema, and set fire to it. P.c. Shepherd was called to the Odeon, where he saw the boys in the manager's office. They admitted taking the ammunition from the shop and two pieces of cordite were found in the pocket of the younger boy. 'I lit a piece in the lavatory of the cinema', he said, 'and my friend lit some and threw it on the floor.' P.C. Shepherd emphasised the danger that might have been caused to the many people

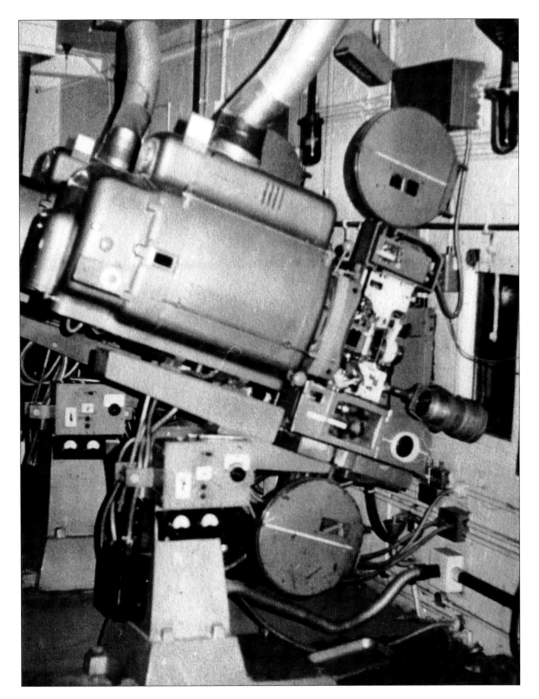

44 *The Odeon's Kalee projectors.*

in the cinema, when the cordite was thrown on the floor. The elder boy, who said he was earning over £3 a week for work in repairing bombed premises, said, 'There's nothing to it, there's only a small light like a match'.

The peak year for attendances was 1948, when 45,000 people saw the film 'The Best Years of Our Lives'. In 1952, Stan Laurel and Oliver Hardy appeared on the stage at the Odeon. The first Cinemascope film presented in Southend, was shown at the Odeon on 7 March 1954, when 'The Robe' was screened. The screen which had been fitted for this presentation was 56 feet wide, and was the first Cinemascope screen to be installed in an Odeon Theatre in East Anglia. This screen could be 'flown' so it did not interfere with the presentation of stage shows.

The café was later converted into Victor Silvester's dance studio. In April 1960 the cinema was renovated and decorated at a cost of £25,000. The seating was reduced to 2,286 to improve the comfort of theatre-goers, by increasing the width between rows from 2ft 6ins to 3 feet. New electric wiring was supplied, also a new sound control system, with special mixing control for the circle. £2,000 was spent on acoustic tiling and modern stage lighting was installed. During the '50s and '60s many fine stage shows were presented at the Odeon, with top stars such Roy Orbison, the Beatles, Cliff Richard and Helen Shapiro.

In 1970, the picture house closed, was gutted completely, and the new twin Odeon theatres emerged: Odeon One seating 455 and occupying the former café area; Odeon Two seated 1,235. The auditorium was formed out of the old balcony, extended forward to increase seating capacity and to provide the new proscenium and screen area. The former balcony foyer became the new entrance hall and pay box location, complete with a licensed bar. The cinema entrance had been moved to the side of the building, in Elmer Approach. The cost of these alterations was £300,000. Under the new cinemas, in the original entrance foyer and stalls area a supermarket was constructed.

Arthur Levenson, known as Southend's 'Mr Entertainment', had been Odeon manager since 1963, although he originally came to the cinema during 1950, as assistant manager. In 1985, he organised the gala 50 Anniversary Night at the Odeon. On 15 July, with a truly great programme which local film fans would remember for many years, Arthur presented a superb evening of entertainment. The film presented was *Return to Oz*, supported by *The Cinema Steps Out* which was one of the 'Look at Life' series. A look at the history of the Odeon was presented by the Westcliff Cine Club's film 'The Odeon Years'. Desmond Llewelyn who played 'Q' in the James Bond films made a personal appearance, with many of the gadgets from the films. But Arthur Levenson had woven some real magic by bringing to the Odeon more than twenty of the Carnival Queens from the past. The 1985 queen Sharon Bourne was crowned by the 1935 Carnival Queen, Catherine Taylor, who had travelled 5,000 miles from Nova Scotia to be at the Odeon.

After the erection of the new Odeon Multiplex, at the top of the High Street, it was impossible for the Odeon to continue, and it closed on 5 April 1997. The last films were *Space Jam* in Odeon One, and *Star Wars* in Odeon Two. The building was demolished in December 2004 and is now partly the site of the University of Essex.

ODEON MULTIPLEX
Southend

Negotiations between developers Odeon Cinemas Ltd (Rank) and Sandfield Lynton and Southend Council for a multi-screen cinema first took place in 1992. The proposed complex was to be built on the site of the former municipal college, at Victoria Circus. After a combination of planning and construction problems, which caused delays, the council finally gave the green light to the scheme in April 1995. By December work commenced on the site for an eight-screen cinema and 11 adjoining shops.

Because of the limited ground area available, owing to the fact it was a town centre site, the picture house was built on three floors, so enabling eight screens to be included in the design. Disabled access was provided to all the auditoriums by lifts or ramps. The total seating capacity of the building was 1,850; the largest screen seated 391 and the smallest 145.

All the auditoriums had draped walls either in rose pink or green and the new design Odeon carpet was fitted throughout the building. Leading off a very spacious foyer screens 1 and 2 were at ground level, with a wide staircase providing access to the upper floors. Screens 3 and 4 were on the first floor and screens 5 to 8 on the top floor. The foyer was decorated in a pastel shade of sea green; also included was blue neon with attractive down lighting, and round opaque light fittings. Six-track Dolby Digital sound was fitted in two of the auditoriums and Dolby Spectral Recording installed in the other six. Luxury seating was fitted in all the auditoriums. Transmitters underneath the carpets meant that the hard of hearing could switch their hearing aids to 'T' and become tuned to the sound wavelength of the film. Also included in the new structure was a café and bar on the ground floor.

Prior to the official opening day, the Odeon screened five days of already released films, which patrons could see for £1 before 7 p.m. and £1.50 after 7 p.m. The cinema was packed, with 4,000 admissions in just one day. At the weekend it was the busiest cinema in the country.

The £10m picture house was officially opened on Friday, 22 November 1996. (It was the first town centre multiplex in Britain.) Attended by many councillors and senior management officials from Rank, the Mayor Howard Gibeon said he believed the new

45   *The Odeon Multiplex cinema in 1996.*

cinema would spell regeneration for Southend. Then cutting through a ribbon of celluloid he declared the state-of-the-art cinema open. This was followed by a gala performance of the British comedy *Brassed Off.*

In February 2000 the Odeon's ownership changed when the Rank Organisation sold its chain of cinemas to venture capital group Cinven.

The gala premiere of the British film *Essex Boys* was held at the Odeon in July 2000. Many stars of the film attended the showing, including Sean Bean, Ray Winstone, Jude Law and Sadie Frost.

During 2004, ownership of the Odeon circuit changed again when both the Odeon and U.C.I. cinema chains were acquired by property group 'Terra Firma'. The Odeon Multiplex has proved a very successful cinema. Film entertainment is alive and well in Southend!

PLAZA
Southchurch

The Plaza cinema opened on Wednesday, 6 March 1929. Situated in Southchurch Road, at the junction of Lovelace Avenue, the theatre was convenient for all parts of the Borough. Both tramcars and buses passed the cinema, just a penny stage from Southend. A car park was provided for patrons adjacent to the theatre. The opening advertisement described the Plaza as a 'Temple of Thespis, an edifice worthy of the district and its residents, where good taste, character and luxurious comfort blended together into a harmonious whole'. The management stated that they felt confident that the residents of Southend East would prefer to patronise the Plaza, because in their midst stood a theatre of surpassing beauty, built solely for their entertainment.

The cinema had a seating capacity of 1,250. The auditorium was decorated in scarlet, gold and mahogany, and illuminated by coloured lamps hidden in the roof. A thick plush carpet had been fitted, with an underlay of felt over an inch thick. The stage had a depth of 17 feet and a 40 feet-wide proscenium arch, which rendered the building easily adaptable for variety turns, and two dressing rooms had been included. The angle at which the floor was raised ensured a clear uninterrupted view from any position. The Plaza had a novel heating system with hot water pipes running between every other row of seats, serving the double purpose of a radiator and foot-rest. The building was complete with a fireproof roof and copper dome. Prices of admission were 6d., 9d., 1/- and 1/3d.

The films on opening night were *The Air Circus*, starring Louise Dresser and David Rollins, directed by Howard Hawks and produced by William Fox. The supporting feature was *The Magic Clock*. Music was provided by the Plaza Operatic Orchestra, with the opening advertisement stating, 'A feast of melody, the synchronisation of the music with the picture is a shining example of the ultimate in motion picture presentation'.

A large and distinguished audience attended the first performance. Mr Herbert A. Manger, the chairman of the company (Plaza Cinema Southchurch Ltd.), congratulated the builders, Messrs. J.C. Flaxman & Son Ltd., on having constructed the building in 24 weeks and having finished the cinema on the day specified in the contract. He also introduced Plaza architect Mr Norman Evans to the audience. Mr Manger stated that although they had not installed a 'talkie' apparatus, they could do so in a very short time, when more such films were available, and when they had achieved a greater popularity. Most 'talkies' were at present variety turns, and he thought most people would prefer to see them on the stage. Mr Manger also paid tribute to the experience of Mr C. Stuart Burgon, the general manager.

Soon after opening it was decided to add sound apparatus, and a R.C.A. Photophone Sound System was installed during August 1930. The first 'talkie' film shown at the Plaza was *All Quiet on the Western Front*, on 1 September 1930.

In November 1938 the following article appeared in the *Southend Standard*:

Cinema Programme Interrupted. During the evening programme at the Plaza cinema, Southchurch, on Friday, a film caught fire in the operating box and the staff promptly lowered the emergency shutters and threw a blanket over the machine involved. Whilst they were dealing with the incident, an announcement of the facts was made from the stage, and a member of the audience, Mrs Tomson, of Roach Farm, Barling, volunteered to play the piano until the programme was recommenced. Her selection of popular airs, including 'The Lambeth Walk', proved exceedingly acceptable and the audience heartily joined in singing the choruses. The Southend Fire Brigade was summoned, but had little to do beyond ascertaining that everything was safe for the show to recommence.

By 1945, the Plaza had become part of the Emery Cinema Circuit. However, between 1948 and 1951 the building was mainly used as a repertory theatre, plays being presented Monday to Saturday (prices of admission were 1/-, 1/6d., 2/6d. and 3/6d.), and film entertainment was retained for Sunday evenings. Seating capacity of the auditorium had now been reduced to 1,225. By 1952 the Plaza had returned to full-time cinema entertainment. Saturday morning pictures called the 'Cowboy Club' took place every week for the children.

On 30 August 1959 the Plaza became the State cinema and a change of film presentation policy took place. Continental and specialised films were introduced, but the new booking

46 *The auditorium of the Plaza in 1929.*

47   *The distinct exterior of the Plaza cinema.*

policy did not prove successful, and three months later on Saturday, 21 November 1959 the cinema closed. The last films presented were *Mighty Joe Young* starring Terry Moore and Ben Johnson, supported by *Where Danger Lives*, with Robert Mitchum and Faith Domergue.

The building was stripped of its cinema equipment and for a while stood empty. Then it was purchased by Hobday Bros, and used as an electrical wholesalers. In 1963, the building was sold for £23,000 to Halsey's Electrical and used for the same purpose. The auditorium walls and ceiling remained unaltered from its cinema days, and were still painted blue and gold. The raked floor, stage and proscenium arch also remained. However, the former rear stalls area had been converted into offices.

Later it suffered a further period of non-use, but the building remained in good condition, mainly because it had been built so well. Newspaper articles in January 1983 gave some ground for hope with the announcement that Southend Arts Council wanted to take over the building, which could include a small cinema, but nothing became of the scheme.

In 1990, the building was purchased by The Christian Fellowship Church, and underwent massive alterations and decoration. In the auditorium the proscenium arch remained but the stage was blocked in. A flat floor was installed and a small balcony added, but the projection box was removed. The former foyer underwent rebuilding, but fortunately the landmark dome over the entrance was kept. The building reopened in 1991, and has since been used as the Christian Church and the Plaza Arts Centre. Still in beautiful condition, it is a good example of what can be achieved with former cinema buildings.

PALACE

Shoeburyness

Shoeburyness gained its own picture house when, on 10 May 1913, the Palace Theatre opened in Ness Road, at the corner of Grove Walk. The opening ceremony was performed by Mr R.J. Banning. A beautiful silver-gilt key, made by Messrs Goodman Brothers, watchmakers and jewellers, of 104 High Street, was presented to Mr Banning to open the cinema.

The Palace seated 500 and was complete with a 24-foot balcony. The building was constructed in brick and rendered in stucco, with a curved pediment to the front elevation. The cinema had a 38 feet wide frontage and a depth of 79 feet. The auditorium measured 60 feet by 35 feet. The word 'theatre' was later deleted from the frontage of the building, and the cinema was just known as the 'Palace'.

By 1917 the cinema was owned by Mr Walter Smith. In 1922 Wilfred Halle was the proprietor and by 1926 control had passed to Mrs Daisy Meatyard. The cinema proved very popular with the nearby Shoebury garrison. A Westrex Sound System was later added for the 'talkies'.

In November 1930 the proprietor of the Palace, William Robert Eve, was summoned to Southend County Police Court because he had a gas meter disconnected in the cinema without giving prior notice to the authorities. Mr Eve said he had the meter disconnected because it was dangerous, as gas had been escaping. If a patron had thrown a lighted match down near the meter, there might have been an explosion. Mr Eve was fined a nominal sum of 5/-.

At a public meeting in 1932, a resolution was passed for the Sunday Entertainment Act (1932), to be extended to the Shoeburyness area, to allow the Palace to open on Sundays, as people from the area had to travel to Southend for their film entertainment on that day of the week.

The lower half of the cinema's frontage was altered during the '30s, to give the building a more modern appearance by the addition of a glazed fascia. At that time the cinema was under the ownership of London and Provincial Cinemas Ltd.

48   *The newly opened Palace cinema, 1913.*

The seating capacity was later reduced to 360.

On 24 December 1946 a large crowd of children eagerly waited outside the cinema, for the arrival of the Mayor and 'Santa Claus' to open the children's Christmas party, which was held at the Palace every year.

The Palace cinema closed suddenly on 5 March, 1955, shortly after the demise of its owner Leslie John Griffin. The last films were *She's back on Broadway*, starring Virginia Mayo and Steve Cochran, supported by *Kid Nightingale*, with John Payne and Jane Wyman.

In February 1956 the Palace was put up for sale by auction. The building was later used as a supermarket and bingo hall, and then for many years as a camping equipment showroom. A false floor had been added at balcony height to divide the auditorium in half. Only the balcony stairs and some of the tiered flooring of the gallery, together with the projection box front, still remained from its cinema days. The exterior, however, was largely unaltered.

The building is at present unused and awaiting redevelopment into flats and retail units, but there is hope that the frontage may be preserved and incorporated in the new building.

49   *After modernisation, the Palace in 1945.*

STAR

Prittlewell

On 22 August 1914 plans were submitted to the building inspection office for the Star cinema. This was to be erected in West Street, Prittlewell, next to the *Blue Boar Hotel*. The owner was Mr W.C. Bradley, of Gladstone House, Hartington Road, Southend. Although the plans were not approved at that time, they were finally passed on 16 March 1915, but the cinema did not open until December 1919. The licensee was Mr James Holloway, from Brighton.

The auditorium seated 430, was 31 feet wide, and had exposed roof support girders, as there was no ceiling. The projection box was above the cinema entrance and pay-box area, entry being gained from a stairway on the right-hand side of the entrance hall. The 10ft 6in wide entrance had a tiled floor and central pay box between the two double entrance/exit doors. The frontage of the cinema was built with a half circular upper façade, rendered in stucco.

Miss F. Bridge recalls:

One Sunday afternoon armed with money intended for Sunday school, my older half-brother took me to the Star cinema instead. We had an orange, a bag of sweets (not popcorn), and an enjoyable time watching an old silent Dr Fu Manchu film, full of horrors. During the film the hero was in mortal danger due to a poisonous snake in his bed. My mother could not understand why, for a least a week afterwards, I would not go to bed unless the sheets and blankets were thrown back first. I never told the boys however!

During its fairly short life showing films the cinema was to have several name changes. In 1920 it became the Priory; the proprietor was Mr H.W. Elston. In 1923 the building was renamed the Gaiety, and Mr B.S. Thomson was the proprietor. In 1925 the cinema became the Ideal. On 22 April 1926 the building then became Gibbs, with Mr S. Clive Gibbs as the lessee and manager. In 1927 an advertisement for Gibbs' cinema stated, 'The music lover's picture house', and 'The cosiest cinema in England'. Programmes were continuous from 2.30 p.m. to 10.30 p.m. To the delight of the youngsters many westerns starring Buck Jones, Ken Maynard and Tom Mix were shown on the Saturday afternoon children's matinées.

50   *The Priory cinema pictured in 1922.*

On 13 December 1928 the building was finally named The Picture House, with Mr H. W. Mead as lessee and manager. The cinema was converted for 'talkies' when a British Acoustic Sound System was installed in January 1931. The auditorium was also redecorated and re-seated, and adverts stated that the cinema was 'the clearest talkie house in the town'. However, The Picture House closed suddenly on 18 March 1931. The last films were *The Arizona Kid*, starring Warner Baxter and Mona Maris, supported by *Life's Mockery*, with Betty Compson.

During 1935, the building was sold for £700, and worked on by a volunteer labour force of about twenty people, including local electricians, signwriters and painters, all of whom gave their services free. The former cinema was transformed into a church in the space of a few weeks, a small balcony accommodating about fifty people was added, and an organ and piano were installed. Part of an internal wall which had been the front of the projection box was removed.

In 1949 the building was leased by the R.A.F.A., although by then the hall was in a rather dilapidated condition, but a number of willing workers cleared the hall and soon had it decorated. Some years later the Southend Amateur Boxing Association took over the hall. It was later owned by the Watney Mann brewery group, who owned the *Blue Boar Hotel*. After being converted into a fitness club, the building was demolished in May 1999, flats being built on the site.

51   *One of the projectors in Gibbs cinema, 1927.*

52   *Interior of the former Star cinema, pictured in 1978.*

CLIFFS PAVILION

Westcliff

The Cliffs Pavilion is the multi-purpose entertainment centre first planned by Southend councillors decades before the project was realised. Entertainment projects for this site go back to 1930, when the plans for a Winter Gardens, with tea rooms, and a Theatre with 500 seats, was one of various schemes over the years intended for this site, which never came to fruition. In 1935, the council decided to purchase the site at Shorefields, and plans were drawn up for a hexagonal-shaped pavilion, estimated to cost £45,329.

Work started on the foundations of the, as yet unnamed, Cliffs Pavilion in 1938, but soon came to a halt because of the deteriorating conditions politically, although £20,000 had already been spent on the project. Through the war and into the early '50s the weeds gained domination over the site. During 1955, work commenced on clearing the vegetation, although it was felt that it would be unwise to anticipate completion of the Cliffs Pavilion before 1957, at an estimated cost of £125,000.

Work on a now larger theatre, with a seating capacity of 1,080, began in 1959. The design was by Borough Architect P.F. Burridge, and the main contractor Gray Conoley & Co. Ltd. The idea was to use as much of the existing foundations as possible from the 1935 scheme. The council debated what the new theatre should be called. Some councillors favoured 'Shorefields Pavilion', but in the end 'Cliffs Pavilion' was decided on.

After further delays, in 1961, pile driving went ahead. During a 21-week period 276 piles were put in. Including the piles which had been put in 23 years previously, coincidentally by the same company, the Cliffs Pavilion would be standing on something like 370 sunken pillars, many of the pillars going down 35 feet, including six or seven feet into the London clay. To achieve this 400 cubic yards of earth had been bored out. The contractors stated that 'the theatre would be the safest building in Essex', and 'it would never move'. The estimated cost for the building had now risen to £322,000. Work now went ahead with the drainage and finally the superstructure.

The theatre was completed in 1964, and the grand opening took place on the afternoon of 4 July. The mayor Alderman E.E. Morris warmly congratulated the Borough Architects

53   *The Cliffs Pavilion in 1992.*

office for their excellent planning, and also the contractors who had worked long hours to complete the building in time for the opening. The mayor then introduced stage and screen actor Bernard Miles, who, after saying how wonderful it was to see a new theatre opening, declared the Cliffs Pavilion open. In the evening there was a gala performance of 'Coppelia' by the world famous Ballet Rambert.

Apart from a couple of shortcomings, the Cliffs Pavilion was much admired by the first night crowds. However there were complaints from the audience at the rear of the auditorium that they could not see. Because the Pavilion had been designed as an all-purpose hall, it had been built with a flat floor. Also it was felt that a considerable amount of sound from the middle of the orchestra was lost in the flies. The first Summer Show commenced on 9 July – this was the 'Norman Vaughan Show'.

The Cliffs Pavilion has presented many different types of entertainment over the years. As well as stage shows and plays, it has shown films, staged boxing, wrestling and snooker evenings, and orchestral concerts, as well has holding antique fairs, presentation dances and exhibitions in the auditorium.

The Cliffs Pavilion closed in August 1991 to undergo an estimated £3 million expansion and refurbishment programme, which would make the auditorium the largest in Essex. With the addition of a balcony the seating capacity was increased to 1,630. A new foyer bar sweeping the width of the building was constructed, offering spectacular views of the Thames Estuary. The main foyer area was completely re-designed to include a new passenger lift to all levels. A mezzanine floor linked the main auditorium with a new Pavilion Restaurant, and a new control room was sited at the back of the stalls. A computerised box office had also been installed. The cost of these alterations finally rose to £4.5 million. To achieve this rebuilding the cinema projection box was removed, thereby signalling the end of film entertainment at the Pavilion.

The new theatre opened on 14 December 1992 with the pantomime 'The Pied Piper of Hamelin', starring Wayne Sleep, Peggy Mount and Richard Marner.

In May 2005 the Cliffs Pavilion's long serving and very successful manager, Charles Mumford, was voted 'Venue Manager of the Year' in a national poll of agents, artist managers and producers, including some of the biggest names in show business. Mr Mumford was also manager of the Palace Theatre. It has been largely due to his efforts over the years that the Cliffs Pavilion has been so successful.

KINGS

Westcliff

The Kings Hall was opened on 7 January 1907. The assembly hall was built behind shops, in Hamlet Court Road, Westcliff. Entry to the hall was by way of a wide covered passageway between these shops. By 1909, the hall had been converted into the Kings Hall Cinema, opening on 5 July, and leased by the National Bioscope Company. The lessee and manager was Mr Arthur Tate.

The opening advertisement stated, 'The Kings Hall has opened for the whole winter season with miles of pictures of up-date-interests. Pictures of adventures and travels, pictures of events in all parts of the world. We put the whole world before you. Comfort, Refinement, Enjoyment with Safety'.

Programmes changed on Mondays and Thursdays, and there were two performances nightly at 7 and 9 p.m., with a children's performance on Saturdays at 3 p.m. Prices of admission were 3d., 6d., 9d. and 1/-, children 2d., 3d., and 6d.

The auditorium was a barrel-roofed hall of great charm, complete with a small gallery and split-level ground floor, which was flat and without any rake. One outstanding feature of the foyer was a cloisonné glass dome, which was inlaid with names of famous composers.

On 22 October 1909 the following article appeared in the *Southend Graphic*:

Mr Arthur Tate has introduced some exceedingly novel effects into his admirable bioscope entertainment at the Kings Hall cinema. He has a machine which can be manipulated to produce sounds representing motor horns, dogs barking, police whistle, fire engine bells, rifle firing, birds, horses galloping, windy day, splashing of water and many other things which help materially to add to the realism of the cinematograph. This remarkable instrument, which has been installed at the Kings Hall, is entirely a novelty and produces from a single source what previously has been the outcome of multitudinous devices and labour.

In November 1910 the following article appeared in the *Southend Gazette*:

People would be surprised how the Kings Hall cinema has taken on a new lease of life, and is a beautiful house of entertainment. Scientifically heated, the hall is the cosiest picture palace in the district. Ever popular pictures, which are changed twice a week, are literally the finest and most up-to-date money can buy.

During 1911 a new and larger screen was installed and the cinema was considered to be one of the most comfortable and attractive halls in the borough. It later gained a café, and the advertisements suggested, 'When shopping in Westcliff visit the Kings Hall café, dainty and light refreshments always available'.

In February 1920 the Kings licence was transferred from Mr S.T. Flatau to Mr Kessler Howes, licensee of the Theatre De Luxe, Southend. The proprietors were now The Kings Hall (Westcliff) Ltd.

On Thursday, 24 March 1921 several buildings in Hamlet Court Road, including the Kings Hall cinema, were damaged by fire. In the cinema the screen, stage, proscenium arch and organ were destroyed. Several front rows of seats were damaged. A new screen was loaned by Harry Garon, proprietor of Garons Imperial Bioscope in Southend Broadway. Men from the Theatre De Luxe, Strand and Garons helped and the cinema was reopened on Saturday, 26 March. The cost of the damage to the picture house was £700.

In, 1923, the cinema was taken over by Ashby's Grand Halls, who closed the picture house for six months. During this time the building was reconstructed and improved. The first step in the process of reconstruction was to knock down the end wall. This was placed much farther back, allowing the seating accommodation to be greatly increased, and also enabling the balcony to be extended. The Kings Hall could now seat more than twice the number of people that it formerly held. Nothing was left of the old hall except the four walls. The roof had been off and the old café demolished completely in the course of the improvements.

An absolutely uninterrupted view from every seat was assured by reason of the new raked floor in the main hall, and the raised flooring in the balcony. There was also no problem with the atmosphere deteriorating as the performance proceeded (as happened in some cinemas in those days), thanks to the new ventilating system which had been installed. Three electric fans drew the impure air out of the hall, and a steady stream of fresh air was constantly drawn in. A point which was emphasised to parents who worried that the health of their children may suffer at the 'pictures'. Any temperature that was required could be obtained, so the cinema could be kept cool in the summer and warm in the winter. Also there was no possibility of any draughts. All the seats were new and so springy and comfortable, that the management felt that, once seated, patrons would not want to get up before the performance was over. The colour scheme of the hall was amber and blue, which was most striking and picturesque. A finishing touch had been added in the form of a series of beautifully decorated lamp-shades, balloon-like in shape, and in a diversity of bewitching colours. The operating room was completely fire proof, and had been fitted with two Kalee 'Indomitable' projectors, with Kershaw arc housings.

The new cinema opened 13 August 1923. Mr H.C. Ashby, the managing director said, 'We have tried to build a theatre that Westcliff will be proud of. Our patrons will get the surprise of their lives when they see the new spacious theatre. They will rub their eyes and ask if this is the place they used to visit a few months ago'.

54 *Interior of the Kings Hall in 1907.*

In May 1932 the cinema was leased out for a year to Mr L.H. Jackson who owned the Mascot, Westcliff, the Plaza at Southchurch and leased the Regal, Southend. The leasing of the Kings Hall enabled the continuation of the Westcliff release of films for Mr Jackson, while the Mascot cinema was being completely rebuilt. On 9 May 1932 the cinema became simply the 'Kings'. At the end of the lease period it again came under the management of Ashby's Grand Halls, in June 1933.

In 1937 the manager of the Kings, Mr W.G. Hudgell, shared with Mr J. Backhouse, of the Kursaal Kinema, the honour of being the oldest-established cinema manager in the borough. He was responsible for the entire running of the picture house, and also booked the films, as the Kings was an independent house. Mr Hudgell came to the Kings Hall in 1922 as chief projectionist. When 'talkies' arrived at the cinema, he wired and prepared the hall himself, and was afterwards congratulated by the inspectors for his work. Although Mr Hudgell later confessed that, when he saw the blue print for the job, which had been sent down to him, his blood ran cold with fright! But he did a good job, as the Kings was renowned for its good sound.

The Kings cinema closed on Saturday, 20 January 1940. The last films were Jack Buchanan in *The Gangs All Here*, supported by Binkie Stuart and Tom Burke in *My Irish Molly*.

55   *After the 1923 modernisation, a completely different Kings Hall.*

In March 1941 the following article appeared in the *Southend Standard*:

A quantity of old films in the rewinding room of the former Kings Cinema was accidentally set alight on Thursday. The dense mass of black smoke that rose, gave rise to the impression that the roof was on fire. Actually the flames and heat did threaten the roof, but the staff threw water on the scene of the outbreak and kept it in check until the arrival of the Fire Brigade.

The hall was requisitioned during the war and used as a N.A.A.F.I. canteen and dance hall for the troops, the cinema equipment having been removed. The building was later requisitioned by the Ministry of Food. In April 1947 it was sold in auction by Mr E.N. Selby for £10,000.

Although the entrance passage still remains, the cinema has long disappeared, the site becoming yet another car park.

PALACE THEATRE

Westcliff

The plans for the Palace Theatre were approved by the planning department on 1 July 1912. Amazingly, compared with modern-day building times, the theatre was erected and ready to open on 21 October 1912, as the New Palace Theatre. Situated in the London Road (then called Leigh Road), at the junction with West Road, the theatre was in a prime position in Westcliff. The total height of the building was 44 feet. The theatre had two balconies and a seating capacity of 1,500. The auditorium decoration and seat coverings were in Rose Du Barry and gold,

The Palace was owned by the 'Raymond Animated Picture Company', and opened with a mixture of vaudeville (which was changed once a week), and bioscope (which was changed on Mondays and Thursdays). The management stated that the vaudeville acts would be high class, with only the best artistes appearing, which ensured the entertainment would be most attractive to ladies and children. Shows were once nightly at 8 p.m. Admission prices were: boxes 10/6d., stalls 1/6d., circle 1/- and 9d., pit 6d. and balcony 4d.

The Raymond Animated Picture Company owned about fourteen other cinemas and theatres. During November 1912 the theatre's name was changed to the Palace of Varieties, but this only lasted four weeks and during December the name was changed back to the New Palace Theatre.

During November 1913 application was made by the proprietors to the Southend Justices for the dramatic licence for 156 performances, to be extended to cover the whole year. The policy of pictures and varieties had all resulted in heavy losses, and it was felt that an unrestricted dramatic licence for 312 performances could turn things around.

The theatre was sold in 1919 for £25,000 to Gertrude Mouillot, who wanted to use the building as a cinema. It was found that the steep rake of the circle made the normal front projection units unusable, so an annexe was built onto the back of the building, and a rear projection system was installed. However, the Palace quickly returned to repertory. In the '20s and '30s the Palace was used by many touring companies.

On Sunday 27 September 1931 thieves broke into the theatre and took away the safe, which weighed a quarter of a ton, from the office of the manageress. The safe contained

56   The New Palace Theatre in 1912.

about £150 and some important papers. It was found abandoned the next day in the River Lea at Hackney Marshes. The back of the safe had been cut into with oxy-acetylene apparatus, and the money was missing. The thieves had obtained entrance to the theatre by forcing a side door leading to the stalls. The door to the manageress' office was smashed, and the safe had been taken downstairs on a trolley. It was then loaded, it was thought, into a lorry.

Between 1930 and 1933 the theatre not only presented the usual repertory, but also had regular film weeks. However films were discontinued on 25 March 1933. The last show was 'Michael and Mary', starring Edna Best and Herbert Marshall, supported by Gordon Harker in 'The Man They Couldn't Arrest'. The Palace reverted to full time repertory with the occasional variety shows.

A new management took over in 1935, and the policy changed to weekly variety bills, with an occasional 'straight' play. However this only lasted to January, 1936, when the Palace closed 'until further notice'. During April 1936 a new lessee, Mr H. Raymond Barrie, a well-known figure in the theatre world, took over the Palace. After reconditioning the theatre with new seats, a new heating system and redecorating the building, Mr Barrie reopened the Palace, reverting to the old policy of once-nightly touring companies, with two shows on a Saturday, which had been a successful formula at the Palace previously.

In October 1937 the Little Theatre Company moved from the Talza Theatre, Southend, to the Palace Theatre, and began presenting repertory on a weekly basis. During 1943, after financial problems had forced the Palace to close, Mrs Mouilott presented the theatre as a gift to the Southend Corporation, who quickly reopened the building. The Harry Hanson Court Players performed the opening play.

The theatre managed to survive the Second World War air raids without suffering any major damage and in 1944 went through a programme of repairs and decorations. Special attention was given to eliminating draughts, for which the theatre was notorious. A new boiler, pump and radiators were installed, to improve heating in all parts of the theatre. The icy wind, which used to rush through the auditorium from backstage when the curtain was raised, now became a thing of the past. Seating in the stalls was re-arranged to give patrons more leg room, so they were not sitting in such a confined space, with their knees almost under their chins. The back circle had always been a box office black spot, because of the poor view of the stage. This area had undergone alterations and was now one of the best positions in the house. The decoration of the walls and ceiling in cream paint had given the theatre a bright and fresh look, and the most up-to-date lighting and sound equipment had been installed.

In June 1956 concern was once again being expressed about the lack of support the Palace was receiving from the local residents. The popular Court Players had departed and, it seemed, a lot of the audience as well. Later, things improved when the lease was taken by Alexander Bridge in 1965 and then later Ray Cooney.

The Palace Theatre Club was launched in 1957, with the idea to raise funds to help keep the theatre open. In 1969, financial problems mounted again and Haymarket Stage Productions announced their final show, 'The Last Laugh'. Then the theatre closed, which set off a massive public outcry. Petitions were organised and protesters marched through the streets of the town.

The Southend Council set up the Palace Theatre Trust in 1970, which registered as a charity and set about establishing a repertory theatre in Southend. Ray Cooney's production of 'Spider's Web' reopened the theatre, which was refurbished in 1973, with help from donations by the council. During 1980, land at the west side of the theatre was purchased, the building was

57   *The Palace Theatre pictured in 1950.*

partly redeveloped, a large foyer and bar area were constructed, and the box office was relocated. A second smaller auditorium was also added, called the 'Dixon Studio', with a seating capacity of 100. These alterations cost £314,000. The building reopened in 1982 as the Palace Theatre Centre, presenting a Gala performance of 'Cabaret'. The Dixon Studio opened in the September of that year with the play 'Duet for One'.

The theatre was rewired in 1986 and, with its 75th Anniversary due the next year, the Palace closed for three months in 1987, and the auditorium was completely redecorated and restored to its former glory at a cost of £120,000. The Yorkshire firm of Bagnalls were contracted to do the renovation. They had been in business for over a hundred years, and had recently restored the Alhambra Theatre in Bradford.

The Palace was repainted throughout, the four boxes with their domes were repaired and restored, as were the chandeliers, some of the seats were reupholstered, the lighting was upgraded, and a new carpet with the theatre's own logo was laid in the foyer. At the finish of the work the theatre looked the same as it did on the opening day 75 years earlier, but with the seating reduced to 603.

To celebrate the 80th Anniversary of the theatre in 1992, resident designer at the Palace, Judy Reaves, spent three weeks designing and painting an Edwardian scene on the theatre's safety curtain. The curtain was 20 feet high and 30 feet wide, and had to be lowered at each performance.

In November 1998 the Palace Theatre Board issued details of a serious cash crisis the theatre was facing. A production of 'Carousel' had suffered losses of £48,000. The Palace closed again in March 1999 and then reopened in the December of the same year. The West End producers Green & Lenagan had been retained to operate and programme the theatre, with Roy Marsden appointed as Artistic Director. The Palace closed again on 29 June 2002, and Green & Lenagan left the theatre without any details being given.

The re-opening took place on 1 April 2003 under a merged management with the Cliffs Pavilion. This proved to be a very successful time for the Palace, with many full houses. Cliffs Pavilion manager Charles Mumford was also in charge of the Palace Theatre, and put together a splendid selection of touring plays, big-name production shows and one-night shows featuring well known performers. Even though the Palace was doing record business, it became a victim of council cuts, and the theatre closed in October 2005 amid a great outcry to save the building. It reopened on 9 December 2006 under the private management of HQ Theatres. The reopening show was the pantomime 'The Wizard of Oz'.

In the latter months of 2009 film shows returned to the Palace Theatre. Special one-night showings of classic films are being presented, with a rear projection unit once again being employed.

Sadly, the Palace has gone through many struggles over the decades, with a lot of openings and closings. It is a building much loved and appreciated by the people of Southend, and continues to this day to provide great and much needed live entertainment.

MASCOT

Westcliff

On 19 May 1913 plans for the Mascot cinema were submitted to the Council planning department by Mr H.A. Barnes, of Cecil House, Clifftown Parade, Westcliff. The plans were approved on 15 July 1913 and work commenced on building the cinema, which was situated in the London Road (then called Leigh Road), on the corner of Beedell Avenue. The owners were Mascot Cinemas Ltd, a freehold company.

The architect was local man Mr Norman Evans, who had succeeded in designing a model picture theatre. The interior was spacious, excellently proportioned and comfortably heated. The diffused lighting was most effective and all the seats were of the 'tip-up' design. In place of the usual orchestra in front of the screen, a musicians' gallery in the centre of the western side of the hall, had the effect of distributing the sounds most agreeably to all parts of the auditorium. The screen was 25 feet by 20 feet, although the proportions of the hall made it look apparently smaller. Heavy curtain screens were erected at the back of the last row of seats. When the floral decorations were completed they added the finishing touch to an elegant and imposing theatre.

The cinema was opened on 12 January 1914 with a seating capacity of 750, which was fairly ambitious for those early days of the bioscope, but it was thought that ample margin had been allowed for development in the area. Admission prices were 3d., 6d., and 9d., children 2d. and 3d. Free teas were provided between 3.30 and 5 p.m. The resident manager was the well known townsman Mr Charles H. Bowmaker, and Mr G. Harland Lann was the musical director. The Mascot became an extremely popular cinema, renowned for its clear and steady picture.

The Mascot closed on 21 May 1932 and was extensively rebuilt. The last films in the original building were *Bought* starring Constance Bennett, supported by *Night Nurse* with Barbara Stanwyck and Ben Lyon. By 1932 admission prices had risen to 7d., 9d., and 1/-.

The lessee of the Mascot was Southchurch Entertainments Ltd, which was part of a chain of cinemas controlled by the L.H. Jackson Circuit, whose managing director was Mr Louis H. Jackson. Four of the original six directors, including Mr Herbert A. Manger, the Chairman, still constituted the board of directors of Mascot Cinemas Ltd. The architect

58 *The Mascot cinema, opening
week, 1914.*

of the new building was again Norman Evans and the builders were local company James
Flaxman & Sons Ltd.

The Mascot was an imposing spacious structure of beauty, dignity and comfort. The
directors of Southchurch Entertainments, together with the architect and builders, had
good reason to be proud of their achievements. The exterior of the building was raised to
65 feet, with the frontage having a central façade rising above two flanking towers, all of
which was finished in 'Snowcrate'. The building had also been extended and expanded from
the original cinema's specifications, especially at the rear of the structure, which had been
achieved by the demolition of the first house in Beedell Avenue.

Above the marble entrance steps and on the lower part of the exterior were artistic
bands of black and white 'Marblexa', running along the whole base of the cinema. This was
an ultra-modern wall-surfacing preparation of extreme durability, composed of specially
treated glass, which being vitrified throughout was impervious to all weather conditions.
The use of this material was further proof of Mr Jackson's enterprise, for the Mascot was
believed to be the first cinema in the country to employ this wall-surfacing preparation.

A pair of illuminated fountains graced the vestibule, on the east side of which a stairway
led to the circle, beneath which was the generating room. On entering the plush auditorium,
it was immediately apparent that comfort and artistic appointment had gone hand in hand.

The walls were decorated in beautiful shades in which gold predominated, the panelling being interspersed by fluted columns. The fibrous plasterwork, undertaken by Brown & Madeley, of Finsbury Park, was a dominant feature of the decorative scheme. It was modern in conception, contrasting broad sweeping lines in Continental fashion with elaborately detailed enrichment.

The bold upright lines that framed the proscenium were reflected in the curved ceiling above, forming one huge semi-circle. Two impressive perforated organ grilles of intricate design adorned the splay walls on either side. Special attention had been paid to the lighting arrangements, resulting in some beautiful effects of illumination, among which the ceiling centres were prominent.

The underside of the circle was designed so that a full view of the screen was obtained from every point. The seating capacity of the new cinema was 1,233. Ample entrances and exits were provided, and the public, managerial and staff accommodation were up-to-date in every respect.

A feature of the mezzanine floor was the charmingly appointed tea-lounge, in which Mr S.B. Kinder, the staff artist, had achieved some striking effects. This embodied a Venetian scene in gold and blue motif, in contrast to the equally charming Old English Cottage tea-room adjoining, in which the atmosphere of picturesque simplicity had been delightfully captured.

59 *Opening week 1932, the rebuilt Mascot cinema.*

60   *Interior of the newly built Mascot, a few days before opening.*

Two large girders weighing eight tons spanned the whole width of the circle which was 51 feet. These had to be delivered to the cinema and fitted into place, between the cessation of the tramway traffic on Saturday night and its resumption on Sunday morning. The length of the auditorium was 108 feet and the width of the proscenium 30 feet. Over the tea room was the operating box, divided from the circle by a fireproof partition. Kalee high intensity projectors had been installed, together with the latest and most efficient R.C.A. Photophone sound equipment.

The Mascot's uniforms for the usherettes were exceptionally smart in beige, with page coats of strawberry and magenta facings, together with silver braid and large berets to match. The male attendants were dressed in French grey whipcord faced with Lido blue and trimmed with silver. The page boys followed suit in French grey whipcord with a Lancer front, and Lido blue with silver.

Mr B. Hodgkinson remembers:

The rebuilding of the Mascot was interesting by reason of the large proportion of the original building that was retained. The contractors used what must surely have been one of the last examples in the area of the old type scaffolding with wooden poles, ropes and barrels. I had just started my professional training at the time and recall the lecturer in the building construction department, at the old Southend night school, sending the class to inspect the project.

The new Mascot opened on 29 October 1932 with the film *A Successful Calamity*, starring George Arliss, supported by Laurel and Hardy in *The County Hospital*, and completing the programme was Frank Darrow in *Dream Mother*.

In 1939 the cinema came under the control of Ben Jay, who also owned the Metropole cinema nearly opposite. The Mascot closed on 9 March 1940 and did not reopen until 14 December 1942. It was then under the ownership of Laurie Cinemas Ltd.

During March 1943 the ownership of the cinema changed again when it became part of Godfrey Cinemas Ltd, but this only lasted to 23 September 1945, when it became part of the Albion Circuit. The next change of ownership took place on 10 March 1949, when it was taken over by John E. Pearce.

A popular feature of this cinema during the '30s and '40s was the café, open daily 12 noon to 8 p.m. (except Sunday), a three-course luncheon was priced 2/3d. During the early '50s Friday evening was 'Mascot Band Show' night with the Bob Kingston Band. This consisted of Bob Kingston at the piano, guitarist Ray Catling, bass-player Alf Page and drummer Geoff Sloman. In the vocal department were Rosemary Nicholas and Lenny Pelosi. The group was later joined by tenor-saxist Pete Bennett. One guest artiste was the singing cinema usherette, Joan Meen.

The Mascot was another cinema to become part of the Essoldo circuit, when on 2 January 1954 they took over the picture house from J.E. Pearce. Ray Catling went on to become chief projectionist at this cinema. The first Cinemascope film shown at the Mascot was

Seven Brides for Seven Brothers, presented on 20 June 1955. In 1961 Bingo was introduced on Sundays.

The cinema's life was brought to an abrupt end on 27 October 1964 by an act of hooliganism which turned the cinema into a blazing inferno. At 11.45 p.m. Mr Schurer, of Beedell Avenue, found he had run out of cigarettes and decided to pop up the road and get some out of a machine. As he neared the Mascot, he looked up and saw there was a blanket of fog over the cinema; then he realised that it was not fog, but smoke! He ran into Westcliff Police Station and raised

61 *The Mascot ... on Fire!*

62   *The remains of the Mascot cinema, the day after the fire.*

the alarm. The Fire Brigade rushed eight engines to the cinema, but within minutes the roof above the stage collapsed with a roar of flame and sparks. The blazing building illuminated the streets, and smoke and flames billowed round the hoarding advertising the film being shown that week, *Ursus in the Land of Fire*, starring Ed Fury, supported by Audie Murphy in *Gunsmoke*.

Employees of the cinema reported that police patrol cars had been called to the building earlier in the evening, because youths had been flinging fireworks around inside the cinema. It was believed one of these was thrown at the screen. It failed to explode immediately and smouldered before setting fire to something on-stage. The building being very old and dry went up like matchwood. When the roof fell in, firemen were battling with the flames from a ladder at the rear of the building. Two firemen fell to the ground with their hoses. Police rushed forward to assist them and were soaked by the hose jets. The firemen were unhurt.

By a quarter to one in the morning police warned the crowd to keep away as firemen were expecting the whole cinema front to collapse. Flames, carried by the wind, threatened the adjoining stores. People living on the east side of Westcliff Park Drive were warned by firemen to be prepared to evacuate. A nearby coffee bar opened up and did a roaring trade.

By one o'clock the whole cinema was a mass of flames and completely gutted. The roof was totally destroyed, and the intense heat destroyed most of the interior. Only the shell remained. Southend's Chief Fire Officer said that in his opinion the cinema was a complete write-off.

The film itself was found undamaged, although some was still in the projectors, and the Bingo equipment was retrieved unharmed from the wreckage and taken to the Coliseum cinema at Leigh. The remains of the Mascot were then demolished. A spokesman from the London office of Essoldo stated that a decision would shortly be made by the directors on whether they would build another cinema. This never came about; instead a shop was built on the site.

METROPOLE

Westcliff

The magnificent new cinema on the London Road, at Westcliff, opened its doors on bank holiday Monday, 10 April 1939. Queues waited to gain admittance to see the Technicolor film *Kentucky*, starring Loretta Young and Richard Greene, supported by Kay Francis in *My Bill*.

The Metropole was owned by Mr Ben Jay, who had a life-long experience in the entertainment world. He had started his cinema career when the silver screen was in its infancy and the possibilities undreamed of. By 1939, he controlled no fewer than ten cinemas, seven of which were at seaside towns. The manager of the Metropole was Mr G.H. Roberts, who had moved to the cinema from one of Westcliff's other picture houses – the Mascot.

Inside the foyer, the charming décor was greatly admired by the opening-day crowds. It had been carried out in tones of jade green, picked out in gold, against a creamy background. The carpets continued the colour scheme, the background being buff, with jade, rust and black intermixed. The male attendants wore uniforms of dark wine red, while usherettes were smartly attired in uniforms of buff, with jade green collars, cuffs and bands on the skirts, and military hats.

63   *The newly opened Metropole cinema.*

64   The Metropole pictured opening week, 1939.

The auditorium was decorated in subdued shades of gold and peach, while a distinctive fluted silk curtain masked the screen. The patrons who visited the cinema on the opening day were unanimous in their satisfaction with the sound and lighting effects, and were sure this cinema would become one of the attractions of Westcliff.

The Metropole was equipped with the latest B.T.H. (British Thomson-Houston) sound system and projectors, with luxury seating, deaf aid appliances and a car park. The theatre was also complete with an air-conditioning system, which circulated fresh air through the building every two minutes. Seating capacity was 1,189 (834 in the stalls and 355 in the balcony), and the proscenium width was 34 feet.

The Metropole closed in July 1940 and did not reopen until 12 July 1942. Because the cinema had been built on land permeated by underground streams, and the front stalls were below ground level, a pump had to be permanently employed to keep the water levels down. When the cinema closed for two years, the pump was switched off, with the result that the auditorium flooded back to the tenth row of the front stalls seats.

The ownership of the cinema changed to Godfreys Cinemas Ltd on 29 March 1945 but this only lasted to 23 September 1945, when the Metropole became part of the Albion circuit.

On 10 March 1948 Mr Herbert Hobden, the supervising manager at the Metropole, was in his office, checking up the day's takings, when two men burst into the room and attacked him. He was struck on the head with a heavy instrument, believed to have been a jemmy. Although badly hurt Mr Hobden fought back, saving the money, and the two men fled. He was taken to hospital and returned to the cinema later with his head swathed in bandages.

The Metropole ownership changed again when it became one of four local cinemas taken over by John E. Pearce, on 10 March 1949. During the early '50s the cinema presented cine/variety nights with the Bob Kingston Orchestra. One such matinée was in aid of Southend's Flood Distress Fund, which had been set up because of the great coastal floods of 1953. The film presented was the premier screening of *The Young Caruso*, starring Gina Lollobrigida. On stage making personal appearances were Stanley Holloway, Joy Shelton and Sydney Tafler.

On 2 January 1954 the Metropole was again one of four local cinemas to change ownership when it came under the control of the Essoldo circuit, the largest independent cinema circuit in the country. They had purchased from J.E. Pearce the freehold of the Metropole and Mascot cinemas at Westcliff, and the leasehold of the Corona and Coliseum cinemas at Leigh. The Metropole did not change its name until Monday, 31 May 1954, when the cinema became the Essoldo, with the erection of giant new name signs on the front and roof of the building. The picture house became the first Westcliff cinema equipped for Cinemascope presentations. The new wide screen was installed by engineers working day and night shifts. In addition the new owners fitted a four-track magnetic stereophonic sound system, the work being completed in time for the advertised 31 May screening of the first Cinemascope film *The Robe*, starring Richard Burton, Jean Simmons and Victor Mature.

During 1971, Essoldo modernised the building at a cost of £80,000 – 650 yards of carpet was just one item. The new luxury cinema in the stalls (the circle was now disused), opened on 22 July 1971 with the film *Paint Your Wagon*, starring Lee Marvin and Clint Eastwood.

On 2 April 1972 the cinema became the Classic, when the Essoldo circuit was part purchased by the Classic cinema group. A year-and-a-half later the building was twinned with a second auditorium, added in the former circle area, which opened on 20 December 1973 with the film *The Aristocats*, a Disney cartoon. The seating capacity was now 423 in Cinema One, which had a pair of 'Fadi' projectors in the operating box. The auditorium of Cinema Two seated 300 and the projection box was equipped with a single 'Westrex' projector, coupled to a tower take-up and rewind system.

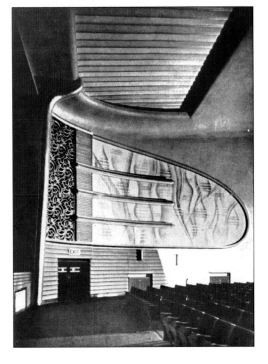

65   *Picturesque auditorium of
the new Metropole.*

Every year a 'Classic Queen' beauty contest was held and floats were entered annually in the local carnivals. Every Friday evening there was a late-night show, which usually ran to a full house. Occasionally there would be an all-night show, which was very popular. 'All Night with Elvis' and 'All Night Hells Angels' were just two of these 'sell out' shows, which started at 11 p.m. and finished around 8 a.m. the next morning. A junior film show was still held every Saturday morning.

During January 1982 a special season of three dimensional films was presented at the Classic. One of these films, called *What the Swedish Butler Saw*, caused a storm of controversy, but attracted such huge crowds it was retained for a second week.

The Classic's long-term manager was Ron Stewart (formerly manager of the Regal, Rayleigh), a very active and dedicated cinema man, who contributed a great amount to the steady patronage and considerable success of this cinema. Ron was named Classic Cinema's manager of the year in 1978, and was in charge at Westcliff for 11 years. The manager of the year award had been won in 1974 by Ron's predecessor, at the Classic, Colin Crosby.

After closing for two days for the installation of Dolby stereo equipment, at a cost of £10,000, Classic One reopened on 18 February 1983 with the film *E.T.* The Classic was the first cinema in the local area to have Dolby stereo.

66   *The Classic in 1978.*

67   *Auditorium of Classic One in 1985.*

On 29 November 1985 the cinema was renamed the Cannon, when the Classic circuit was purchased by the Cannon Film company. A year later Cannon went on to purchase the A.B.C. cinema circuit, which meant they now had a cinema in Southend. For a few years Cannon ran both cinemas, but then decided they did not want two picture houses in the same area, and, although the former Classic was still making money, as the smaller cinema of the two, the decision was made to close the Westcliff cinema.

Amid tearful scenes the Cannon was closed on 21 February 1991 and Westcliff lost its only cinema, the last films were *Kindergarten Cop* in screen one, and *Cinema Paradiso* in screen two. Queues built up for both films at least an hour before the last show; all seats were taken in screen two and nearly all in screen one. On a very emotional evening, the staff, together with former staff members and friends, gathered to say a sad farewell to the cinema. 'We have nothing to celebrate,' said projectionist Derek Dorking. 'We have no idea why we are being forced to close. We have a loyal and regular clientele, and our takings are healthy.' Chief projectionist Paul Clarke said, 'I am heartbroken. To see this fine cinema close and to have built up equipment over the years only to see it scrapped is heartrending. I have thought seriously about leaving the business'. Cinema manager Theresa Crosby stated, 'We have a band of devoted regulars. There are people who come here every week who are saying that they cannot believe we are closing'. Theresa transferred to the Southend Cannon cinema as assistant manager.

The building was demolished in September 1994 and another fine cinema was lost forever. Halfords store now occupies the site.

CORONA

Leigh

The Corona cinema was built in Leigh Road, Leigh, on the site of a pottery, just a short distance from the *Grand Hotel*. It was designed by Westcliff architect Mr James Saunders and built by the well known local builders Messrs. James Flaxman and Sons Ltd. Construction began in April 1929. The exterior had a simple dignity and imposing proportions (a frontage of 90 feet), the interior an atmosphere of homeliness and unobtrusive luxury.

The exterior was a red-brick structure, substantial rather than ornate, relieved by Bath Stone dressings and a white marble entrance, with bases of polished black marble. The Oregon pine entrance-hall and adjoining café were enriched with Carrara marble, the hall being paved with vitriegated marble. An illuminated cockle shell surmounted the façade.

The spacious and lofty interior, which had a seating capacity of 1,530 on a single floor, was delightfully restful and inviting. The decorative scheme was artistically carried out in royal blue and old gold. These shades were repeated in the handsome drop curtain and other draperies, which shimmered like the sea. To commemorate the local fishing industry, a maritime design was interwoven into both the interior and exterior of this unique picture house. In the auditorium the fibrous plasterwork colourfully displayed the cinema's sea-faring theme. Fish, crabs, shells, lobsters and sea-gulls were all present. The cinema had a 38-foot-wide elegantly designed proscenium arch which continued the maritime theme, and was flanked by beautifully designed organ grilles, where again the maritime element was in evidence. The surmounting galleons were a reminder of how Leigh's Elizabethan past had played a conspicuous part in meeting the menace of the Armada. The walls had hand-painted landscapes by Miss M.C. Dendy of Hadleigh.

The Corona's lighting installation provided effects of a novel and beautiful character, which were controlled from a huge switchboard weighing one and a quarter tons. Owing to the fact that the whole of the electricity supply was generated on the premises, many exclusive effects were achievable. Large transparent shades reflected light of any desired tone upon the ceiling panels. Not only was the auditorium flooded with a diffused glow of appropriate colours, but dawn, sunset and other such effects were available.

The ventilating system controlled a perfect supply of incoming sea air, heated to the required temperature. The inner air was extracted by powerful four-foot fans. A special wall covering had been applied to the auditorium to ensure perfect acoustics. The orchestra enclosure was spacious, the centre being occupied by the two-manual console of the Christie organ, built by William Hill & Son, and Norman & Beard, of London. Dressing rooms and an orchestra room were provided beneath the stage. Kalee projectors had been installed in the operating box, together with the latest British talking-picture apparatus.

The owners of the Corona cinema were the South-Essex Cinema Syndicate Ltd, the directors of which were well known members of the local community, including Frank Baker, managing director of the Warrior Square Picture Theatre, at Southend. The cinema had cost £23,000 to build.

The Corona was opened on Saturday, 19 October 1929 at 2.30 p.m. Admission prices were 6d., 9d., 1/-, 1/3d. and 1/6d.

The *Southend Standard* reported:

Quite quietly, unheralded by speeches or presentation of bouquets, the new Corona cinema switched on its beautiful lights, sounded an organ note of triumph for work well done, opened its doors and let the patiently waiting queues of the expectant public in. A row of directors,

68   *The Corona cinema, 1929.*

and the resident manager Mr Lawrence Kemp could be observed and looked well pleased. They had good cause, for the opening of such a place, with the thousand and one technical details to be attended to, might cause anxiety to those concerned, and some setbacks might be excusably anticipated. As it was all went well. The central heating did its work adequately, a detail which was acceptable on a chilly afternoon. The beautiful lighting effects changed constantly, and the 'Japanese Sunshade' ceiling lights were admired by all. The curtains ran smoothly and the talkie apparatus was excellent.

The show commenced with the Corona orchestra, consisting of eight performers, under the direction of Mr Vernon S. Kirby, who gave selections from their repertoire.

The picture programme consisted of a newsreel followed by a 'talkie' comedy, 'At the Dentist', and a short coloured film. London organist Harold W. Howell then played a selection on the massive Christie organ, and this was followed by the main film, *The Devine Lady*, starring Corinne Griffiths and H.B. Warner.

The *Southend Times* reported:

A crowd of close on two thousand people nearly caused a tram stoppage outside the Corona, on the evening of the opening day. Crowds lined both sides of the street and there was a queue 100 yards long. Not for many a long day – if ever – has Leigh witnessed such a site. One naturally expected a good crowd, but nobody could have anticipated how all the world and his wife rolled up to stand in line outside, or to watch those who participated in this ordeal of patience.

69 *The auditorium of the Corona on opening day.*

70 *Section of the auditorium's fibrous plasterwork.*

Passing tram cars and motor traffic had to slow down to negotiate the assembly and the effect was seen in more ways than one. Adjacent tradesmen found business so gravitating into their shops that they rubbed their hands with glee and, naturally, hope the new era will continue. The addition to our amusements may be a welcome quickening factor to the life of Leigh. Even the compliment paid to Leigh by the decorative inclusion of the illuminated cockle shell high in the cinema's façade had an irresistible home appeal.

The resident organist at the Corona was Mr H. Williams, whose theme tune was 'Cockles and Mussels'. For a number of years the programmes included variety/cine evenings.

On 5 May 1937 the Corona became part of the Mistlins Theatres group. On 29 March 1945 the picture house was taken over by Godfrey Cinemas Ltd, whose control only lasted until 23 September 1945, when the announcement was made that the cinema had become part of the Albion Circuit. This lasted until 10 March 1949, when the Corona was taken over by John E. Pearce. The auditorium seating capacity had been reduced to 1,429.

The next change of control came on 2 January 1954, when the Corona became part of the Essoldo circuit. During November of that year, the cinema was redecorated and Cinemascope was installed, the auditorium being equipped with a screen 36 feet wide and 15 feet high. *The Robe* was the first film shown in this format, on 29 November 1954.

Essoldo remained the owners of the Corona until the cinema's closure on 4 April 1959. The last films were *Seven Brides for Seven Brothers*, starring Jane Powell and Howard Keel, supported by Tom Ewell and Anne Francis in *The Great American Pastime*. After remaining empty for a while, there was hope that the building would become an indoor bowling green, but the cost of £20,000 to buy and convert the building prevented this.

In 1964, efforts were being made to convert the former cinema into a Bingo Hall, but the Town Planning and Building Committee refused consent, later confirmed by the Council, because they felt it was inappropriate to the area. The building was used by a soft drinks distributor, and later by other various commercial retailers. In 1982 the former cinema became a snooker hall. Since then the building has been divided by the addition of a floor, and a bowling alley was installed upstairs.

EMPIRE PALACE
Leigh-on-Sea

Early in 1910, a cartoon appeared in the *Southend Graphic* newspaper of John Mitchell with a cinema projector, and underneath the following caption, 'A scheme is on foot to construct a building for Bioscope Pictures, and probably also a skating rink, on the land which has been acquired by Mr Riches, of the *Grand Hotel*'.

Built on this land in Leigh Broadway, the Empire Palace cinema was opened on 3 December 1910. The auditorium seated 400, and on the first night a full house saw

71   *The Empire Palace in 1910.*

72   *Full house at the newly opened Empire Palace.*

the film *The Heads of the World*. Owner, Mr John Mitchell, told the audience he intended lengthening the building, if it was well supported.

A month later the *Southend Graphic* newspaper reported:

Thanks to Mr John Mitchell, of San Remo Parade, Westcliff, Leigh has now its own picture palace, and a very bright and comfortable place of entertainment it is. The carefully selected programmes are enhanced by the inclusion of vocal turns, with new and original songs expressly composed by Mr Mitchell. *We Shall Never Live Today Over Again*, has created quite a furore. Special attention has also been paid to the heating of the Empire Palace.

The building was without a ceiling and had exposed curved iron roof support girders. There were several rows of forms at the front of the auditorium, known as the 'tuppenny forms'. Although by later standards the building was a small picture house (the land had a frontage in the Broadway of 60 feet, and the auditorium had a length of 75 feet), the Empire Palace was considered a very respectable place of entertainment. During 1911, at great cost, special arrangements were made to show film of the Boat Race, Football Cup Final, Derby and the Coronation of King George V, on the same day as the actual events.

In February 1912 Mr Mitchell kept his opening-day promise. The auditorium of the Empire Palace was enlarged to provide for the accommodation of a further 250 people. The ever increasing attendances at the popular cinematograph hall had made the extension to the building necessary. The enlarged cinema was ready by Easter (5 April).

During the First World War the cinema was opened for free shows for the soldiers. The usherettes wore black frocks with white aprons, and from time to time sprayed the auditorium with Jeyes Fluid from special containers. Mr Dickenson played the piano, which was augmented in the early evenings by two violins and sometimes a drum. In the early '20s the cinema name was changed to simply the 'Empire'.

In mid-December 1930 the cinema closed for installation of the latest talking picture apparatus. The building was re-decorated and the auditorium re-seated. The lessee and manager was Reginald Burton and one of the projectionists Lawrence May. The Empire reopened on Friday, 26 December with the greatest musical comedy of the year, *Sunny Side Up*, featuring the well known stars Janet Gaynor and Charles Farrell.

On 5 May 1937 the cinema became part of the Mistlin's Theatres group. The Empire survived until 9 December, 1937. The last films were *Dodsworth* starring Walter Houston and Ruth Chatterton, supported by Cicely Courtneidge and Max Miller in *Things Are Looking Up*. The building was later used as a garage, and various retail shops, finally being demolished in February 2009. Plans have been approved by the council to build flats on the site.

HENRY'S HALL

Leigh-on-Sea

Mr Henry Bridge was a well known local carpenter and builder, who had built many houses in the Leigh area. He lived near the Broadway in Leigh Hall Road. In 1909, Mr Bridge purchased some land on the south side of the recently planned out Maple Avenue, which connected to the Broadway (previously called Leigh Lane). This land had been part of the Leigh Hall Estate, which was sold in 1893 for development.

In March 1910 there were newspaper reports of plans being drawn up for a proposed new concert hall and skating rink, which shortly were to be erected at Leigh. The interested parties were not identified, and no further reports followed for two years.

In the meantime Mr Bridge submitted plans for a shop, furniture repair works and living accommodation to be built on the land he had purchased in 1909. The plans were approved by Leigh District Council on 7 November, 1911, and the building was erected by early spring 1912. It was situated on the corner of Maple Avenue and the Broadway, with its frontage on the Broadway. The local architects were Charles Cooke and Son.

In May 1912 Mr Bridge applied for consent to convert his shop, etc, into a concert hall on the first floor and a furniture auction room on the ground floor. After initial rejection by the council, the plans were modified and then gained approval.

The roof of the building was fitted with an early type of air-conditioning system, which pumped air through the building, and stopped the build up of stagnant air in any section of the structure. It also stopped gases accumulating under the floors. Water also had to be constantly pumped out from the footings, because the building had been erected in an area of watery fields and ponds.

Named 'Henry's Hall', on the front of the building was a small balcony on which Mr Bridge and leading members of community and council, including the Mayor, gathered on the opening day, 8 June 1912. The opening ceremony was performed by the Rector, the Rev. R.S. King, who was also the chairman of the urban council. The Rev. King congratulated Mr Henry Bridge upon having designed and erected the splendid building. After the opening ceremony a concert was given under the musical direction of Mr William C. Crooks.

Leigh's newest place of entertainment was open, with seating for 600. On opening day, the first show was an attractive presentation of magic and mystery by Keith Syko (billed as 'the last of the wizards'), and Dot Irving (billed as 'the extraordinary clairvoyant'). Local people would no doubt recognise the entertainers as the well known local poet, John Keith Sykes, and Mrs Sykes, who had both appeared at the principal London and provincial halls.

Prices of admission were, afternoons at 3 p.m., 3d. and 6d., children 1d., evenings at 8 p.m. 3d., 6d. and 1/-, children 2d. On 22 June, the Leigh Dramatic Society presented their production of 'Caste'. The building continued as a concert hall for some years, but its limited seating capacity did not help with the booking of star performers. On a non-regular basis bioscope shows were presented, but these were discontinued by 1915.

In 1923 the building was taken over by Dossett's bakery and an extension was added to the side of the building. Dossett's kept the building right up to the late '80s, and then it became the Midel Cleaning Supplies store. In 2004, application was made for the development of a five-storey block of flats,

73   *The opening of Henry's Hall, 1912.*

which did not find approval with some of the local residents. In 2011 the building was empty and waiting demolition.

COLISEUM

Leigh

The Coliseum cinema was built in Elm Road, Leigh, on the former site of Dr Watson's residence. Situated in an ideal location at the tram terminus, this picture house was to provide Leigh film enthusiasts with the epitome of comfort and luxury. The proprietors were Watson and Broadhurst, and the architect Mr Frank Bowhill. Originally plans had been passed by Leigh Council for a cinema on the east side of Elm Road, near the junction of Pall Mall, which were later withdrawn when Dr Watson's site was purchased. Plans for the new site were deposited with the Building Inspectors Office on 14 November 1913 and approved on 17 February 1914.

74 *The Coliseum cinema, opening week, 1914.*

75   The auditorium of the Coliseum in 1914.

The cinema building had a lot of charm, with a barrel ceiling and plush upholstered seats, mounted on a single sloping floor, at such an angle that people sitting in the back rows could view the pictures without craning their necks, in spite of hats in the rows in front. The auditorium was decorated in gilt and red, and had a seating capacity of 600. The stage was adorned by potted palms on either side of a 'roller blind' covered in current advertisements for O.K. sauce, etc. There was an orchestra, but no organ. The cinema opened on 11 April 1914. Performances were continuous from 2.30 to 10.30 p.m., admission prices were 3d. and 6d., children 2d. and 3d. During 1918, the Coliseum was sold to Mr Charles Dare.

In October 1928 plans were being drawn up for major alterations and rebuilding of the Coliseum. The architect was Mr E.A. Stone, the well known London theatre designer, and the builders were Messrs. F.J. Green & Sons, of Elm Road, Leigh. The Coliseum was completely altered and enlarged to accommodate increased audiences for the 'talkies'. The roof was raised 20 feet, while performances continued, the cinema closing only when interior work began. An upstairs foyer and large balcony were added, increasing the seating to 1,100. The rake of the floor and the tiered floor of the balcony ensured a perfect view from every point. The screen equipment was such that the stage could be adapted for variety acts within a few seconds. The colour scheme of the auditorium was a restful shade of old gold, the walls being treated with art plastic, surmounted by a ceiling of mottled blue. This colour was also employed in the handsome curtain and hangings.

The cinema frontage, which was finished in Atlas white cement, was classic in design and of massive and simple outline, yet so proportioned that the effect was imposing without being heavy. The green bronze decorations of the canopy and window frames enhanced the artistic effect. The original marble entrance hall remained (with a new semi-circular entrance), the walls were decorated in polished walnut, the hall was spacious and inviting. A perfect system of ventilation had been installed, controlled by electric fans, which provided a continuous supply of pure air, adequate in cubic air space for each patron. Western Electric sound equipment had been installed, embracing both the 'disc' and 'sound on film' systems, coupled to Simplex projectors. The boiler for the heating system was located in a heating chamber at the stage end of the building, the various radiators being fed by pipes in trenches beneath the floors.

Because the original cinema had been so popular, the new one was not received with favour by all. Many people felt it had been enlarged to hideous proportions, and that the exterior resembled an austere cenotaph. The new picture house opened on 25 January 1930 with the film *The Trespasser*, starring Gloria Swanson. The original architect Frank Bowhill and his wife Nell emerged from the opening night looking very depressed.

A spool of the film, *The Gay Divorce*, was destroyed by a small fire in the operating box at the Coliseum on 2 July 1935. The audience was asked to leave the cinema when the outbreak occurred. However, within 20 minutes the audience had filed back in and the show was running again, after the Leigh section of the Southend Fire Brigade had quickly

76 *Completely altered, the rebuilt Coliseum in 1930.*

subdued the flames. No damage was done to the operating box or the building owing to the safety shutters in the box itself.

It can only be a measure of the general feeling towards the new cinema that, six years after the rebuild, on 14 November 1936 the Coliseum closed again for a further transformation. The cinema had been leased to Messrs, Knight, Cohen and J. Rafer on 27 September.

The cinema reopened on 26 December 1936 with the films *Everybody Dance*, starring Cicely Courtneidge, supported by Alice Brady in *The Harvester*. The famous Odeon architect George Coles designed a new interior for the Coliseum in the art deco style. It was a beautiful auditorium, with a proscenium width of 26 feet, and the seating capacity increased to nearly 1,500.

The following report appeared in the *Southend Times*:

> Like a phoenix from the ashes, the Coliseum has arisen in all its splendour with only the name as a reminder of the past. The foyer looks charming with its scheme of Cerulean Blue and Pillar-Box Red lines. Elaborate interior decorations delight the eye when the lights are up, and the luxurious appointments include seats devised on the lounge chair principle, with Dunlopillow rubber arm rests and specially shaped full length backs, upholstered in a delicate shade of pink crushed mohair velvet, that tones with the general colour scheme of coral pink, beige and reseda green, with touches of orange to brighten the effect. New carpets have also been fitted. The pendant lights have opal shades so the effects are bright without being dazzling. The ceiling colour is terra-cotta sprayed with gold. The proscenium arch is screened with coral pink silk velvet curtains. Every modern convenience has been utilised in the re-building, even to the twin heating and ventilating plant, which purifies the air every thirty minutes, dispersing germs in a manner that is essential to the well-being of the cinema-minded public. In addition to this, a highly efficient and smart staff have been engaged by the enterprising management, whose intention it is to study the needs of their patrons from every possible angle. Usherettes will be attired in attractive original uniforms of the French artist type, trousers replacing skirts, soft blue silk blouses and chic berets, worn by a bevy of pretty girls. New 'talkie' equipment has been installed. The manager Mr V.F. Theobalds, is to be congratulated on his up-to-date methods in forwarding the aims of the fast growing circuit owned by Messrs. Cohen and Rafer, who, with the reopening on Boxing Day of the Coliseum, will have added another striking achievement to their already long list, as has architect Mr George Coles. Admission prices are 6d., 9d., and 1/- in the stalls, and in the circle 1/4d. and 1/6d.

On 12 May 1937 the Coronation broadcast was relayed to the Coliseum between 10 a.m. and 12.30 p.m.; every seat for this special presentation was free. At 8 p.m. the Kings speech was included in the programme. The Coliseum was the only cinema in the area to show film of the Coronation on the same day. Other picture houses in Southend showed the films the following day.

The new cinema proved very popular with all the patrons. A good orchestra was retained for intermissions with the 'talkies', but eventually had to give way to recorded music. On 29 March 1945 it was taken over by Godfrey Cinemas Ltd, but the control of the cinema changed again on 23 September 1945, when it became part of the Albion Circuit. The next change came on 10 March, 1949, when the cinema was taken over by John E. Pearce.

The staff of the Coliseum spent their off-duty hours during December 1950 constructing a large Christmas tableau, which was erected on the canopy of the cinema. The general

77   *After closure as a cinema, in 1986 as Sterlings Bingo Club.*

manager Mr R. Craven organised a competition among his staff for the best idea for a Christmas tableau. The ideas were pooled and the final tableau depicted a Dutch scene with two electrically operated windmills, which were illuminated.

Having taken over the lease from J.E. Pearce, the Coliseum was another of the local cinemas to come under the control of the Essoldo circuit on 2 January 1954. Films were discontinued on 22 May, 1965, when the building closed as a cinema. Mr Harry Lamber, Essoldo's general manager, said, 'We have been running the Coliseum at a loss for so long, business was very poor. We cannot see a future for it as a theatre, it is just not wanted in the area'. The last film presentation was Rock Hudson and Doris Day in *Send Me No Flowers*, supported by *I'd Rather Be Rich*, starring Sandra Dee.

The building was then converted into the Essoldo bingo club, later becoming Ladbrokes 'Lucky Seven' bingo club, and then Sterlings bingo club, which finally closed in January 1997. For a short time it was used as a teenagers' night club. Then, during a period of closure, many ideas were put forward for the future of the building. These included reopening as a cinema, conversion of the building into an arts and crafts centre, or conversion to a café/bar, with a stage area for hire by amateur groups.

Instead of any of these ideas finally coming to fruition, partial demolition of the former cinema took place in October 2001 and the shell of the building was converted into shops and flats.

KINGSWAY

Hadleigh

The Kingsway cinema was a large, imposing and palatial structure standing on a magnificent site on the north side of the London Road at Hadleigh. It was built by a local labour force employed by Messrs. M.E. Stanton Rolls, of 14 Victory Parade, Sutton Road, Prittlewell. The land where the cinema was constructed was sold to Kingsway Cinema (Hadleigh) Ltd, of which Mrs Rolls was co-director, with Messrs. F.A. Rolls, P.T.W. Stanton and H.B. Shenton. They were not only responsible for the cinema, but had also previously built and opened shops in Hadleigh and Thundersley. Plans for the building had been passed by Benfleet Urban District Council on 26 February 1935. It was the first purpose-built cinema in the Benfleet urban area. The fast increasing population of the district had now reached 13,000.

The building was a landmark sited in the main shopping area, and the cinema would become the most splendid place of entertainment for miles around. For months it had been the centre of interest during its construction. By October 1935 the neat white notice board announcing, 'Site for Super Cinema' had been replaced by something much more tangible in the shape of a giant steel framework. The structure would also include a restaurant and dance hall to accommodate 400 people. The architect was Mr Leslie C. Norton, of Albemarle Street, London.

The Kingsway was opened on 27 April 1936. Queues stretched from the entrance down the side of the cinema and right round the car park. Patrons were provided with two car parks, one at the side of the cinema, the other opposite, and both were full to capacity.

Those who were inside were gratified to find a really super cinema. The auditorium was built on the stadium design, with a seating capacity of 1,500. The interior was decorated in golden brown, red and gold, with blue splashes. The proscenium arch was 40 feet wide, with the curtains coloured in shades of gold, silver and blue. The stage had adequate accommodation for occasional variety shows to supplement the screen entertainment. The lighting effects were of the diffused type, being both brilliant, and at the same time restful, and in all parts of the cinema blended in perfect taste with the furnishing and pastel decorative scheme. The seats were of the latest design, with Sorbo rubber arm rests and ample leg room. Deaf aids

78   *The Kingsway cinema on opening day, 1936.*

were fitted to certain seats. The fresh air system made sure the temperature in the auditorium was correct, the air was cleaned and afterwards extracted at regular intervals. Impressively, 800 feet of neon had been used on the exterior of the structure.

79   *The magnificent Kingsway before the opening ceremony.*

The 7 p.m. opening ceremony was a little late to allow as many of the crowd in as possible. When the curtains rose they revealed two small pages holding a long tape in front of the platform party. Mr H.B. Shenton, the managing director, first apologised for the delay, and then introduced Major-General George Mathew, C.B., who congratulated Mrs Rolls on a splendid building, which he hoped would stand for many generations as a tribute to her public-spiritedness. They might also congratulate themselves on having Mr Shenton as manager, for his wide experience would always provide a first-class show. He asked everyone to join him in wishing the adventure every success. Miss Betty Fields, sister of Gracie Fields, then cut the tape and declared the cinema open, and wished Mr and Mrs Rolls every success which, she felt sure, the lovely theatre deserved. Mr Shenton presented a beautiful bouquet to Miss Fields, on behalf of the directors, and a representative of the Kingsway Parade of shops presented the same to Mrs Rolls, who said she knew how much the people of Hadleigh needed a cinema, and that they wanted it more quickly than it had been possible to provide it, but everyone had done their best.

Mr Claud Gardiner, famous as a member of the 'Air-Do-Wells' Concert Party, then took to the floor for a few moments with a couple of stories, and the curtain rang down on a laughter-filled house. A second later there was cheering as the first film for public presentation was flashed on the screen. The Kingsway Cinema was open and the programme had begun! 'Pathe Magazine', a colour symphony and Norman Foster in *Behind the Evidence*, an American gangster film, followed one another, before the stage show, in which the Kingsway Dancing Girls showed their worth in a variety of numbers, matching their talent against an old hand, Joe Boganny and his Crazy College Boys, not forgetting the dog, Bonzo, whose all too-lifelike antics brought the house to a state of collapse. The Kingsway organist, Miss Peggy Webber, gave a short recital, demonstrating both her own ability and the beauty of tone of the mighty Compton organ. The organ was equipped with the Compton 1936 tonal effects, called the Electrone, which lent itself to a wider variety of uses, such as the most famous carillons or the Westminster chimes to be reproduced with fidelity. Then followed the feature film, *Jack of All Trades*, starring Jack Hulbert and Gina Malo. Prices of admission were 6d., 9d., 1/-, 1/3d. and 1/6d.

For many years the Kingsway was leased by the Associated British Cinemas circuit. During 1951, the latest Western Electric projection and sound equipment were installed. The big news of 1955 was the cinema being fitted out for Cinemascope, the first presentation being *Sign of the Pagan*, shown in week commencing 11 April.

The Kingsway closed on 16 January 1959, when the A.B.C. lease came to an end, but reopened on 7 December 1959 as an independent cinema. First musicals and family programmes were presented, but after a time these gave way to a season of Continental and 'X' certificate films, but finally the management booked films which had already been shown in Southend. Film transport costs had to be a consideration with all suburban cinemas.

Since 1949, Mr Gus Keeling had been manager of the Kingsway, a man absolutely dedicated to that cinema, whose experience and enthusiasm in no short measure helped to keep the Kingsway open, battling the effects of television. He had left the Kingsway for a year when A.B.C. gave up the cinema, but returned when Mrs Stanton-Rolls reopened the cinema independently.

80   *The Kingsway's stadium style auditorium.*

During the '60s, as well as film entertainment, the cinema presented Old-Time Music Hall, All Star Variety, Bingo, Boxing and Wrestling. Many top stars of the wrestling world appeared at the Kingsway, including Mike Marino, Judo Al Hayes, Ski Hi Lee and the masked Doctor Death. The ballroom was hired for a time by the Western School of Dancing, which had dance classes every night of the week.

The cinema finally closed for film entertainment on 26 February 1965. The last film was *Goldfinger*, starring Sean Connery. The building remained open for wrestling tournaments every fortnight. Mr Keeling stated, 'The cinema is being forced out of existence by the big cinema companies, who release some of the best films, but will not let independent cinemas like the Kingsway have them until they have been round the whole circuit. The last film we showed was *Goldfinger*, which had been well worn by Southend cinemas within easy reach of Hadleigh residents'. Mr Keeling added that he was very sad to be leaving the district, but he had received several good offers of managerial posts from various cinemas in the country and had been released to accept one of them. Mrs Stanton-Rolls said she hoped the cinema would not be closing for good.

The building lasted until 1970 and was then demolished. The Compton organ had been removed and installed in the recreation hall of Dalys House, part of Rochford Hospital. When much of the hospital closed, the organ was transferred to the Red Brick Barn, at Rochford, owned by farmer Charles Tabor. The barn has been converted to hold concerts, and has a seating capacity of over a hundred.

A supermarket was built on the site of the Kingsway, but for some time now the building has been unused.

THE RAYLEIGH CINEMA
Rayleigh

On the left side of Bellingham Lane, off Rayleigh High Street, stood a large house in the late 1800s, where Mrs Bellingham lived. The house faced the High Street and later became Miss Colliers School for Young Ladies. Just past the school, and running alongside the lane was a hall, which formed part of Miss Colliers School. The girls used this hall to perform shows and pantomimes.

When the school closed, the building was taken over by two of Rayleigh's businessmen and the hall was converted into a cinema called the 'Rayleigh Cinema'. The owners were Bert Thomas, a sign writer, who had learnt cinema projection work, and Ernest Clayton, an estate agent.

The hall was a brick building which included a café. Films were projected from behind the screen on a rear projection system. Programmes ran daily from 2.30 p.m. to 10.30 p.m. Prices of admission were 5d., 9d. and 1/2d. The afternoon price was 6d. anywhere, and children 3d. before 3 p.m.

During 1930, talkie equipment was installed. In 1931, the cinema was renamed the Cosy and prices were increased to 6d., 9d., 1/- and 1/6d. The Cosy lasted until autumn 1936, when the owners, the Bostock circuit, closed the cinema and demolished it to make way for the Regal.

81 *Monthly film programme booklet for The Rayleigh Cinema.*

REGAL

Rayleigh

The Regal was erected on the site of a previous picture hall, called the Rayleigh Cinema (later renamed the Cosy), in Bellingham Lane, Rayleigh. The Regal was built in 1937, by local builders Messrs W. French. The cinema had an overall depth of 138 feet, and the width of the frontage, which faced out into Bellingham Lane, was 63 feet. It was originally owned by the Bostock Circuit.

The Regal opened on 29 April 1937. The cinema had a very picturesque auditorium with a seating capacity of 696, on a single level, and a proscenium width of 39 feet. One member of staff at that time was young Herbert Warner, who looked so proud in his page's uniform. By 1945,

82   *The Regal, 1973.*

the cinema had become part of the Radion circuit, owned by Mr B.E. Fortesque. In the early '50s the Regal was part of the Bentley circuit. It later passed to Mrs R.F. Webster and was finally purchased by Astoria Films (London) Ltd. Cinemascope was installed in November 1955.

Upon leaving school at the age of 15, in 1945, Mr Ron Stewart started work at the cinema as a trainee projectionist. It was to be the beginning of a long and very successful career at the Regal, which culminated in October 1968, when Mr Stewart was appointed manager of the cinema.

83   *The auditorium of the Regal cinema.*

During March 1970 the Regal applied for a bingo licence, and there were fears for the future of film entertainment in Rayleigh, but these fears proved unfounded as Bingo never arrived.

The Regal was one of the last family-owned cinemas in the area, and was renowned for the personal service approach towards its patrons. One example of this was a Christmas Eve, when two little girls trudged through the snow to see *Cinderella*. They were the only people in the auditorium, but the Regal ran the film for them! This cinema building had a very homely feel about it. Ron Stewart always stood at the entrance to welcome his patrons, and likewise to bid them goodnight at the end of the performance.

In July 1971 the Kalee 8 projectors with B.T.H. arc housings, which had been installed when the cinema was built, were replaced by Kalee 21's, because spare parts were becoming unobtainable for the old projectors, but in all those years they had only suffered one mechanical breakdown. The manager and his projectionist worked through the night to install the new equipment. Mr Stewart recalls, 'Replacing the old projectors meant another sentimental link with the past had disappeared. The same had happened with the cinema cat, over the years several patrons had walked off with our cats'. Right to the end of the cinema's life Ron still ran a very successful Saturday Morning Pictures Show for the children.

In September 1973 the closure of the Regal was announced. The proposal was for shops, offices and a new cinema to seat 300 to be erected on the site. The picture house closed on 29 September with the films *Dirty Harry*, starring Clint Eastwood, and Jane Fonda in *Klute*. The contents of the Regal were sold and the building was promptly demolished.

Despite petitions from local residents, a new cinema was never built. Offices were built on the car park area, and a block of one-bedroom flats named 'Homeregal House' were erected on the former cinema site.

RIO

Canvey Island

The Rio cinema was built in Furtherwick Road, Canvey Island, and opened on Whit-Monday, 1 June 1936. It provided the island residents with a form of long-needed entertainment. The owner and proprietor of the Rio was Colchester businessman Francis Bertram.

The cinema had been decorated with extreme delicacy throughout, in pastel shades of grey, white and cerise, which was enhanced by the splendour of the lighting arrangements with polished metal electric light fittings. The seating capacity was 1,000 in comfortable armchair seats on a single-level raked floor. The proscenium width was 25 feet, and Kalee projectors with Vulcan arc housings had been installed in the projection box.

On opening day, long before opening time, a large queue built up along Furtherwick Road, which ensured there was not a vacant seat at the opening performance, and a large waiting company assembled outside the cinema for the next house. Many leading residents of Canvey were present. Mr Bertram was accompanied on the stage by the Chairman of the Canvey Island Urban District Council, Mr J.E. Longman, and Mr George H. Chambers (its former Chairman), who was due to perform the opening ceremony.

After the formal introductions, Mr Longman expressed the pleasure and delight they all felt being able to meet on such a notable occasion in Canvey's history. He added that everyone knew Mr Chambers had been connected with the life of Canvey for many years, and his opening of the cinema that day was just another landmark in the work he had done for the Island over the years.

Mr Chambers responded by saying that they were in Canvey's first purpose-built cinema, and he thought that they could fairly claim that its opening marked another stage in Canvey's progress. He also thanked Mr Bertram for producing a building which they must all admire for the exquisite taste that had been displayed in its design.

Mr Chambers said that it was a great achievement for Mr Bertram to have designed and built it himself, all with local labour, from plans he had drawn up himself in his own office. He added that whilst the cinema was in no way built on the ambitious lines they found in the large towns, it was a cinema provided for Canvey and suited to its every need and requirement. That was what Mr Bertram had set out to cater for, and they must admit he had exceeded their expectations in the magnificent building he had given them, with ample accommodation and its replete fitting up throughout. He told the audience that the air they were breathing had been washed and filtered before they received it, as required by the County Council regulations, though why they should want that with the Canvey air he failed to see, knowing its purity and beneficial qualities. Mr Chambers added that it was an admirable building and just suited to what the Island required. It was now up to the people of Canvey to make it a success. He then declared the cinema open.

The opening programme consisted of a Pathe 'Gazette', followed by a short film about Hollywood film production and the famous studios, next there was a comedy short called *Vocations Laze*, and to complete the programme the feature film *Broadway Gondolier*, starring Dick Powell and Joan Blondell. Patrons leaving the cinema said how remarkably clear the picture had been and how good the clarity of sound was in every part of the house. Admission prices were 6d., 1/-, 1/3d. and 1/10d. (reserved). There were two performances daily (not continuous), except Saturday when there were three houses.

During a safety inspection in September 1944, 32 gallons of petrol were found underneath the cinema by the police. Apparently because there was a high risk of petrol being stolen at the start of the war, it had been stored in a safe area under the concrete floor of the Rio and then forgotten.

In the mid-'50s Cinemascope was installed and later the projectors were changed to B.T. H. Supa's. In the '60s, the ownership of the Rio changed to Mr Charles Craythorn, whose company was called Craydem Cinemas. The seating capacity of the cinema was reduced to 588, and the proscenium area of the auditorium widened and modernised, and a larger screen was fitted. Bingo was introduced in 1965, on Monday and Thursday evenings, but the Rio always had Saturday morning film shows for the children.

In May 1976 the following article appeared in the *Canvey News & Benfleet Recorder*:

Rowdies help put bingo in at the Rio. The Rio is the latest screen casualty. It is to make way for Bingo. 'Rowdy youths are partly to blame', says manager Mr George Stevenson. 'There were no point customers going to the cinema on Friday and Sunday nights hoping to enjoy the film because of the row created by youths. The noise is awful. When we showed 'Please Sir' the other Friday it was chaos. There was a full house, but these lads

84 *The Rio cinema.*

85   *Interior of the Rio after the installation of the Cinemascope screen.*

just wouldn't be quiet'. Mr Stevenson added, 'On Fridays I employ two bouncers, on Sundays three. They patrol the aisles and when their backs are turned they get apples thrown at them. One Friday night twenty ash trays were ripped from the seats and the toilets lost their chains. Bingo will take a lot of worry off my mind'. But money is also a prime mover in the change, on a Wednesday night recently, the net profit was only £2.10, the 'X' films do make money. Mr Stevenson said, 'We had one a few weeks ago and I did terrific business, but I prefer the family entertainment and they just don't make those kinds of films anymore'. Bingo will be permanent from 3rd June, but the cinema will be open for children's matinées in the school holidays.

The Rio closed for film entertainment on 29 June 1976. The last film was *The Mickey Mouse Anniversary Show.* This was not the only local cinema to lose patrons through rowdy behaviour, but what these youths gained from contributing to the closure of one of their own places of entertainment I cannot imagine.

The building was renamed the Canvey Leisure Centre. National bingo chain Seldis Cooper bought the club in April 1998 and spent £300,000 on refurbishment, lighting and state-of-the-art equipment, making it the best equipped in Essex. The name was changed to the Rio Bingo Club.

Mr Seldis said, 'We have brought back the community spirit and the club is serving the community again. People who remember the club as it was will remember an old rat hole, but now it is a palace, complete with air conditioning, a bar and a snack bar'.

The building is still open as a Bingo and Social club.

MOVIE STARR

Canvey Island

Plans for a four-screen cinema complex were passed by Castle Point Council in April 1997. The proposed cinema involved the conversion of an amusement arcade in Eastern Esplanade, on Canvey Island to provide the entrance to the complex. A large extension would then be built at the rear to house the four auditoriums. The council felt the cinema would provide a valuable facility for the people of Canvey, fairly near the town centre, but also sufficiently away from residential areas.

86   *The Movie Starr Cineplex in 1998.*

The owners and developers were the Alpha Leisure Group, who also had to provide a car park opposite the cinema site. A competition was held for film fans to guess the name of the new cinema, which was being kept secret. The winner would receive free tickets to the cinema for six months.

By November 1997 construction of the cinema was well under way. It was hoped the building would be ready to be opened by Christmas, but this was to prove a little optimistic. The eagerly awaited cinema name was revealed: it would be called the Movie Starr Cineplex (the previous amusement arcade had been called the Starr Play).

The cinema was opened on 19 March 1998 for public viewing, with films commencing the next day. The Cineplex had a total seating capacity of 446. All auditoriums

87 *Ernie Johnston in the projection box at the Movie Starr Cineplex.*

were air-conditioned and had luxury seating installed with extra leg room. Seating was also provided for the disabled and a special sound induction loop for the hard of hearing. Two of the auditoriums were structured with tiered seating and two with raked flooring. A cloakroom was provided and a computerised ticketing system. The state-of-the-art cinema was fitted with Dolby digital sound systems in screens 1, 2, and 3, and Dolby S.R. (Spectral Recording), in screen 4. The communal operating box had four Century projectors with 'Strong' long-play film platters. The seating capacities were screen one 138, screen two 122, screen three 111 and screen four 75. The opening films were *The Man in the Iron Mask*, *The Full Monty*, *Titanic* and *Amistad*.

The Movie Starr Cineplex is the modern success story of our local cinema history. Projectionist Ernie Johnston has been with the cinema 11 years and before that was projectionist at the Rio cinema for a quarter of a century. Ernie says, 'A lot has changed in the cinema-going experience in 40 years, most cinemas don't have the curtains which used to cover the screens in years past. It made the cinema, gave it character and added to the presentation'. He recalls, 'In those days you had to work with two projectors, which you kept swapping between every 20 minutes, now everything is more high-tech'.

But Ernie Johnston is a projectionist from the 'old school', constantly checking the focus of the film, the sound levels and even the temperature in the auditoriums, making sure a visit to the Movie Starr Cineplex is a great night out.

Cinema Name Changes

SOUTHEND

Rivoli: Empire Theatre, A.B.C., Cannon, New Empire Theatre.

Kursaal: Ruffels Imperial Bioscope, Kursaal Kinema.

Princes Picturedrome: Princes Hall, Avenue, Lyric.

Pier Hill Cinema: Southend Picture Palace, Grove Picture Theatre.

Theatre De Luxe:

Gaumont: Hippodrome Theatre, Gaumont Palace.

Garons: Garons Imperial Bioscope.

Gem Electric Theatre:

Strand: Kinemacolor Theatre, Warrior Square Picture Theatre, Essoldo.

Regal: Arcadia Theatre, Ambassadors' Theatre, Regal Theatre.

Civic News Theatre: Talza Hall Theatre, Talza Theatre, The New Repertory Theatre, The New Vic, The Continental.

Ritz: Top Rank Bingo Club, Invicta Bingo Club.

Odeon: Astoria, Odeon Twin Theatres.

Odeon Multiplex:

SOUTHCHURCH

Plaza: State.

SHOEBURYNESS

Palace: Palace Theatre.

PRITTLEWELL

Star: Priory, Gaiety, Ideal, Gibbs, The Picture House.

WESTCLIFF

Cliffs Pavilion:

Kings: Kings Hall.

Palace Theatre: The New Palace Theatre. Palace of Varieties.

Mascot:

Metropole: Essoldo, Classic, Cannon.

LEIGH

Corona:

Empire Palace: Empire.

Henry's Hall:

Coliseum: Essoldo Bingo Club. Lucky Seven Bingo Club, Sterling Bingo Club.

HADLEIGH

Kingsway:

RAYLEIGH

The Rayleigh Cinema: Cosy.

Regal:

CANVEY ISLAND

Rio: Rio Bingo Club, Canvey Leisure Centre.

Movie Starr:

INDEX